Designing and Implementing Effective Evaluations

Designing and Implementing Effective Evaluations provides extensive real-life examples of program evaluations that illustrate the various elements and steps in conducting a successful evaluation. The detailed and diverse range of case studies shows the common elements, methods, approaches, and processes of program evaluations, while also demonstrating the way that good evaluators adapt and tailor those methods to the specific characteristics and needs of a given program.

The chapters explore the process of problem solving while navigating multiple stakeholders, competing agendas, and varying environments. The book introduces conversations concerning how to adapt evaluation processes and concepts with culturally different individuals and communities. It discusses the role of culture in navigating a meaningful evaluation process when significant cultural differences exist between the evaluator and individuals that make up the organization.

The text is a vital resource for postgraduate students in Program evaluation courses in Psychology, Education, Public Health, Social Work, and related fields.

Steven D. Kniffley Jr., PsyD MPA ABPP, is Spalding University's Chief Diversity Officer, Associate Professor in Spalding University's School of Professional Psychology, and Coordinator for the Collective Care Center Racial Trauma Clinic. His area of expertise is research and clinical work with Black males and the treatment of race-based stress and trauma, and he was selected as one of Louisville's top 40 under 40 for 2020.

Kenneth J. Linfield, PhD, is Professor Emeritus at Spalding University, Louisville, Kentucky, where he has taught the Program Evaluation course in the doctoral program for the past 13 years. He has been involved in the CASE Collaborative – an international group of evaluators working to promote the use of cases in evaluation teaching and learning.

Designing and Implementing Effective Evaluations

Comprehensive Case Studies in Program Evaluation

Edited by Steven D. Kniffley Jr., Kenneth J. Linfield

LONDON AND NEW YORK

Cover image: TBC

First published 2023
by Routledge
4 Park Square, Milton Park, Abingdon, Oxon OX14 4RN

and by Routledge
605 Third Avenue, New York, NY 10158

Routledge is an imprint of the Taylor & Francis Group, an informa business

© 2023 selection and editorial matter, Steven D. Kniffley Jr., Kenneth J. Linfield; individual chapters, the contributors

The right of Steven D. Kniffley Jr., Kenneth J. Linfield to be identified as the authors of the editorial material, and of the authors for their individual chapters, has been asserted in accordance with sections 77 and 78 of the Copyright, Designs and Patents Act 1988.

All rights reserved. No part of this book may be reprinted or reproduced or utilised in any form or by any electronic, mechanical, or other means, now known or hereafter invented, including photocopying and recording, or in any information storage or retrieval system, without permission in writing from the publishers.

Trademark notice: Product or corporate names may be trademarks or registered trademarks, and are used only for identification and explanation without intent to infringe.

British Library Cataloguing-in-Publication Data
A catalogue record for this book is available from the British Library

ISBN: 9780367229627 (hbk)
ISBN: 9780367229726 (pbk)
ISBN: 9780429277788 (ebk)

DOI: 10.4324/9780429277788

Typeset in Times New Roman
by Apex CoVantage, LLC

Ken: "I dedicate this book to my brother, Roger Paul Linfield, in memoriam. His stellar career as an astrophysicist, his relentless pursuit of excellence in hiking and peak bagging, rock climbing, birding, and wood cutting, and his enduring involvement in my children's lives will live on for all who knew him. He set the bar for me in mathematical precision, which was a primary factor in my journey to Program Evaluation. We miss you, Roger."

Steven: "This book is dedicated to my son, Justice, and my life partner Brittney. Brittney without your immeasurable support I would not be the person I am today. Justice, you inspire me to break through glass ceilings each day so your possibilities will be limitless. I also dedicate this book to those upon whose shoulders I stand including my hero and father, Steven Kniffley Sr."

Contents

List of Illustrations viii
Foreword ix
Contributors' bios xii

1 Introduction to the Book   1

2 Negotiating the Complexity of Context in Evaluation   8

3 Professional and Interpersonal Competencies in an Evaluation
   Capacity Building Collective Impact Project   27

4 'Dream big, believe in yourself, and keep moving forward'
   ManaiaSAFE Forestry School Pilot Kaupapa Māori Evaluation   43

5 The TCS School Program Evaluation   57

6 Leveraging Cultural Humility in the Evaluation Process to Facilitate
   the Healing of Organizational Trauma   64

7 The Path to the Future   74

8 Reflecting on the Cases and Looking Ahead   88

Illustrations

Figures

2.1	Visual showing the two groups of children for analysis	24

Tables

2.1	National Institute for Early Education Research Program Quality Benchmarks	11
2.2	Cast of Characters	20
2.3	Students Eligible for Study	25
4.1	MFS Pilot Evaluation Summary of Questions and Methods	47

Images

2.1	Non-equivalent groups of children	22
2.2	Equivalent groups of children	23

Foreword

Kenneth J. Linfield
Steven D. Kniffley Jr.

I (Ken) still marvel at the developments that brought about this book. The idea began in August 2018 when the 9th edition of *Program Evaluation: Methods and Case Studies* (Linfield & Posavac, 2019) made it into print. Although I had doubled the number of case studies compared to the 8th edition and expanded all of them to include the same seven Program Evaluation elements (Meeting needs, Implementation, Stakeholders, Side Effects, Improvement focus, Outcomes, and Nuances), it still seemed that greater elaboration of real-life examples of program evaluations could be a useful addition to helping students learn. My colleague Dr. DeDe Wohlfarth had recently published a book of case studies in child and adolescent psychopathology (Wohlfarth & Morgan, 2017), so I imagined that there might be a similar need in program evaluation. I asked my Routledge editor at the time if there might be a market for such a book, and she replied that there certainly should be, and Routledge would be willing to look at a proposal for it. In what would become a theme, I figured I knew what to do and I got started.

A number of the first steps still seem like fine ones in retrospect. I knew that there were important areas where others knew much more than I, so I approached Dr. Steven D. Kniffley Jr. about co-authoring such a book. I am very grateful that he was willing to join me in the project. We talked about key goals and ways to reach them, especially including explicit elements about cultural humility and addressing the many aspects of culture related to both evaluands and evaluators, areas of Steven's expertise. We put together a proposal and sent it to Routledge.

As we were developing the proposal, we were aware that we would not be creating a manuscript unaffected by the increasing focus on systemic injustices occurring across the country. This growing awareness contributed to folks seeking opportunities for reflection and dialogue to better understand the sociohistorical challenges facing marginalized communities. We wanted to put together a document that underlined the importance of individual and organization cultural reflection as part of the evaluation process. As organizations seek to facilitate more inclusivity in regard to policies, hiring practices, new ventures, and other transformational changes, we wanted to provide examples of evaluators working across the spectrum of diversity as they navigated challenges throughout the evaluation process. By including these types of cases, we believed that the reader would be more equipped to address the challenges of an ever increasingly diverse world.

While we were waiting to hear back, I received an invitation for a webinar being presented by the International Society for Evaluator Education (ISEE). When I had attended the recent American Evaluation Association conference, I mentioned my interest in getting more involved in groups connected with evaluation to several folks. I was not exactly sure who might have passed along my name and interest, and I did not remember hearing specifically about ISEE at the conference, but I was pleased to have this chance to dip my toes in the water. Little did I realize just what an opportunity was being offered.

As the webinar began, I felt my jaw drop (although I tried not to show it on camera). The presenter talked about using case studies as an important element in teaching Program Evaluation. Although I knew better, it felt like the webinar had been planned just for me. I had no idea there were others who focused on this area. As things finished up, someone asked if anyone might be interested in following up on the topic. I eagerly added my name.

From the first meeting of the group, which grew into the CASE Collaborative, I had two powerful and recurring reactions. One was that I regularly thought "This is wonderful! These people are interested, even passionate, about this exciting area that I care about." I looked forward to the virtual meetings, and I would finish them with a kind of glow. I would tell my wife and friends, "I had another CASE meeting today! They are such a great group!"

But my other reaction was thinking, "I don't know anywhere near as much about using Program Evaluation case studies in teaching as I thought I did." Other members talked about educational theories and strategies that I sometimes recognized but could not have explained fully. Some folks referred to multiple courses and workshops and other trainings, and I was still teaching the one course on Program Evaluation that our program offered. Although I worked hard to keep up with the conversations and to make some kind of contribution, I felt like I was always running to try to catch up with the others. On the one hand, it was exciting to be a part of such a knowledgeable and accomplished group. On the other hand, I had some sense of an imposter syndrome – that I didn't belong with these others who knew more and did more than I.

Still, our conversations were highly productive. We talked about differences in cases along various lines. Some were best described as "exemplars" – examples of particular evaluation elements, whereas others presented challenging situations or raised questions. By building up to a decision without revealing what others had done, students could think through possible choices and talk together about how to handle these kinds of difficulties. I realized that I had only thought of cases as exemplars, so the group had vastly expanded the range I expected.

We began to talk about how some cases are highly comprehensive, providing details on most if not all aspects of what happened, whereas others provide a much more limited account of one piece of an evaluation. The more complete narratives present a much richer picture with details that flesh out the settings, the people involved, and the ways things developed, and these offered students many good insights into the complex world of evaluation. There are times when a small snippet can address a more limited but still appropriate objective of a given lesson, such as illustrating specific concepts like changing the goals or methods of an evaluation because of changing circumstances or new information. The collaborative agreed that "Big-C Cases and small-c cases" was a good way to note the differences among the various versions that were still all cases.

Our first venture was a multi-paper session at the American Evaluation Association conference in November 2019 – "Using Cases to Cultivate Competency Development and Responsible Practitioners." We presented our ideas about what makes a case as well as why and how to use cases as an essential part of educating competent evaluators. Our subsequent conversations set out a plan for multiple projects, including an issue of New Directions for Evaluation – "Case-centered Teaching and Learning in Evaluation" (Kallemeyn et al., 2021).

Dr. Kniffley and I soon realized that the CASE Collaborative members were some of the most knowledgeable folks to write about evaluation cases, so we invited the members to become a part of this project. Although some were not able to join us for various reasons, we were blessed with those who did. Unfortunately, COVID and other complications repeatedly prevented still others from contributing, so this modest initial contribution to the field, shorter than we originally hoped, may especially serve as an incentive for others to build on it.

In all, I am enormously grateful to those who helped make my naïve venture so much more productive than it would have been without their contributions, especially to the members of the CASE Collaborative. In many ways, my best advice to readers is to let this book be an introduction to the great work of the Collaborative that I expect will become more and more central to using Cases in evaluation education.

Kenneth J. Linfield
Colorado Springs, CO
June 2022

References

Kallemeyn, L. M., Bourgeois, I., & Ensminger, D. C. (Eds.). (2021). Case-centered teaching and learning in evaluation. *New Directions for Evaluation, 172.*

Linfield, K. J., & Posavac, E. J. (2019). *Program evaluation: Methods and case studies* (9th ed.). Routledge.

Wohlfarth, D., & Morgan, R. K. (2017). *Case studies in child and adolescent psychopathology* (2nd ed.). Waveland Press.

Contributors' bios

Elissa W. Frazier, conducts school improvement program evaluation at Education Development Center (EDC) with extensive experience in urban education. She is an Ed.D candidate at Loyola University Chicago currently researching culturally responsive practices and digital equity in K12 with a specialization in organizational evaluation.

Dr. Leanne Kallemeyn is an Associate Professor in the Research Methodology department at Loyola University Chicago's School of Education. She teaches courses in program evaluation, qualitative methodology, and mixed-methodology. Her research interests include teacher's data use, qualitative inquiry and evaluation methodologies. She has been the principal investigator of multiple evaluation projects in the education field and is currently participating in the CASE Collaborative.

Mr Henry Koia (Ruawaipu). (Diploma in Māori Business Graduate Diploma in Strategic Management). MFS Evaluation Project Manager and Executive Director, Train Me Quality Services Limited trading as ManaiaSAFE Forestry School, Te Tairawhiti, Gisborne, Aotearoa New Zealand.

Bianca Montrosse-Moorhead, PhD, is an Associate Professor of Research Methods, Measurement, and Evaluation at the University of Connecticut. As an evaluation researcher, educator, and practitioner, Dr. Montrosse-Moorhead specializes in evaluation methodology, theory, practice, and capacity building. Her research focuses on improving evaluation quality, evaluator education, and applied studies of policies and educational interventions designed to promote student learning and educational equity.

Ms Christine Roseveare (Master of Public Health, Diploma in Teaching, Fellow Higher Education Academy), is a lecturer at Massey University - Te Kunenga ki Pūrehuroa, Aotearoa New Zealand where she teaches an evaluation course to undergraduate health science students. She is an award winning teacher with a long time interest in using case studies to help students learn.

Dr. Jay Wade is an evaluation and evaluation capacity building practitioner who specializes in creating shared measurement and evaluation systems for nonprofits and foundations. He is currently the Executive Director at Planning, Implementation & Evaluation (PIE) Org in Chicago, IL, where he serves over 50 organizations annually on multiple research and evaluation projects. His primary work is with foundations and community collaboratives, coaching large dockets of nonprofit grantees to streamline evaluation measures and outcomes reporting. Dr. Wade is a former child therapist and a part time faculty member of Loyola University Chicago's School of Education, where he teaches evaluation and research methods.

Jennie Weiner is an Associate Professor of Educational Leadership at the University of Connecticut. Her scholarship aims to re-frame educational leadership and change to make both more inclusive, equitable, and oriented toward collective uplift. This includes a focus on naming and disrupting gender and racial discrimination in the education pipeline and in leadership specifically. She has published over 40 peer-reviewed articles and is the author, with Dr. Isobel Stevenson, of *The Strategy Playbook for Educational Leaders: Principles and Processes*. Teaching is her passion.

Dr Marg Wilkie (Ngāti Porou, Ngāpuhi) is a Kairangahau Matua (Senior Researcher) with the Research Centre for Hauora and Health at Te Kunenga ki Pūrehuroa Massey University in Aotearoa (New Zealand). With 25 years as a kairangahau Kaupapa Māori, working in Māori higher education and health, including Kaupapa Māori evaluation. Currently co-designing an evaluation of a mātauranga Māori (knowledge) based project that is one of the first indigenous models of cancer care of its kind in the world.

1 Introduction to the Book

Kenneth J. Linfield and Steven D. Kniffley Jr.

Introduction

Welcome to this book of cases in Program Evaluation – well elaborated, well fleshed-out, and well detailed. The use of cases, sometimes called case studies, as an important component of teaching and learning has a well-established history – dating back at least to the 1920s in Harvard University's School of Business, at which point they noted that the Law School had already used the approach for 25 years (Jackson, 1926). One common motivation for using cases has been recognizing the vital difference between abstract concepts and concrete examples, especially for those learning a professional practice. For example, in many professions, there is a commitment to promoting fairness or justice, but exactly what is involved in making things more just or fairer may seem very different to different people. A story about someone who made certain choices such as sharing the income from a project with those who participated in it provides a clear example of a specific approach that would not be as obvious if only the general idea of working for justice were presented. Someone who agrees in theory with justice might be adamantly opposed to the idea of sharing income as a way to demonstrate justice. Alternatively, someone else might be more strongly supportive of such a practice than the more abstract idea of promoting fairness.

There are now instructors in a wide range of disciplines who use cases as part of their classes, and many programs either encourage the use of cases as a common technique or even center the entire curriculum around the use of cases. In addition to Harvard's Law School and Business School noted earlier, cases have been used in a very wide range of fields, including Education and Social Work programs, (Austin & Packard, 2009), Clinical Psychology (Wohlfarth & Morgan, 2017), Management Information Systems (Kawulich, 2011), and Music Methods (Richardson, 1997). In training for medical doctors, Grand Rounds have been a long-established specific case-based educational approach (Elstein et al., 1990). Many other educational programs have also used cases as an important component of instruction.

In particular, there has been a growing recognition recently in the field of evaluation that cases are a very useful technique for helping students learn important elements. The issue was raised in a preliminary way in 2005 in an issue of New Directions for Evaluation (Patton & Patrizi, 2005), but has been developed more fully in another issue of the same journal recently (Kallemeyn et al., 2021). Some now suggest further that case-based teaching is a "signature pedagogy" – an essential component not only for novices but also for experienced practitioners who want to develop advanced skills. (Montrosse-Moorhead et al., 2021).

DOI: 10.4324/9780429277788-1

Teaching and Learning

One of the points that many advocates of using cases emphasize is that it is essential to think about the processes of both teaching and learning when considering productive approaches. The two are necessarily connected – teaching only makes sense when there is someone learning what is taught. But it is possible to concentrate too much on one side, such as focusing on particular techniques, styles, or elements of teaching without reference to the exact settings, learners, and other aspects of the specific context. In contrast, a balanced approach to teaching and learning recognizes that the two elements always interact. A teaching approach that worked well on one occasion might not work well with others, not because it is a universally bad approach, but because it is not a good match for those other learners. A productive teaching and learning process requires a good match between the teaching elements and the learners.

Among other things, there is a very wide range of aspects of teaching and learning. The level of the learning matters – what works for those just being introduced to a field is likely to be very different than for those who have been involved for years and are looking to develop advanced skills. A related point is the specific goal or purpose of the teaching and learning. It is important early in evaluation classes to introduce basic concepts like logic models – noting that evaluators work to learn what elements of a given program are included with the intention that they will lead to particular outcomes. When such points are being introduced, relatively simple examples that illustrate the basic ideas are appropriate. Later, when addressing more complex issues such as what should be considered sufficient evidence to support a given logic model, a more advanced example or set of examples, such as looking at the specific results of inferential statistical tests on the data collected regarding a given logic model, address the more sophisticated issue of what evidence is good enough.

Other aspects of the particular setting are also highly relevant. Evaluation classes in an evaluation curriculum or program require different approaches than a single evaluation class that serves as a minor component or even elective in a program with a different focus. To make things even more complicated, different students in a given class may have different agendas from their classmates, so that a tightly focused form of instruction may miss some or even many of the students.

One of the goals for the cases in this book is to provide an especially wide range of different elements that lead to many different ways to use them to match a broad variety of learners. Such a goal means that some readers will gain particular points from this book and other readers will gain different points, even if there is substantial common ground as well. Readers will certainly notice many aspects of the variation in the cases. Among other elements, the chapter on the ManaiaSAFE Forestry School program illustrates this range both by following the Māori writing convention of presenting the Māori words first, followed by the English translation, and by using the English conventions that are often referred to as the UK style, which are the standard in New Zealand. Although it is common to have all chapters in a book follow the same conventions, the different style of Chapter 4 is an explicit example that any given case is different from all other cases in some important ways. Some of the details about the various ways that cases are different are explicitly noted in the cases, while other details are provided just for the instructors in the online resources.

Context and Culture

Building on the differences with regard to teaching and learning, an important theme in this book is paying attention to cultural elements that are a part of evaluations in a very broad sense. The specific culture of the evaluand – the project and the people involved in it – is a vital consideration for good evaluators. Competent evaluators cannot work effectively with any program if they do not understand these essential components. As Wilke, Rosavere, and Koia note in their chapter, the Māori community involved in the ManaiaSAFE Forestry School program held a number of specific Māori values and priorities. Those values and priorities in turn had a number of important implications, such as their much greater collaboration with "Dr. Marg" than if the evaluator had no Māori connections. Likewise, as Montrosse-Moorhead and Weiner indicate in their chapter, the values and priorities of the Foundation for Science and Mathematics affected the director's choices in important ways. The evaluators made adjustments to their plans to accommodate those choices in the best way they could. The reader will see various examples of how the culture of the evaluand affected important elements in each of the cases.

One crucial first step in competent evaluations is learning the various cultural realities of the program, its staff and other stakeholders, and related aspects of the setting. In recent years, there has been a growing awareness of the many dimensions of culture – race, ethnicity, gender, sexual orientation, socioeconomic status, and much more. Increasing proportions of those who identify with majority or dominant cultures have discovered that they tend not to notice many of the elements that contribute to their own privilege, while those on the other side of privilege are regularly aware of them.

This point highlights another aspect of culture – the cultural elements and perspective of the evaluators. Just as teaching and learning are two descriptions of an integrated process, the cultural perspectives of both evaluators and the evaluand interact in any evaluation. Good evaluators do not just need to learn details about the culture of the evaluand. It is essential that they understand their own cultural perspectives so they can recognize how those perspectives help or hurt their work with the particular culture(s) of the evaluand. Very affluent evaluators who simply knew that the clients and staff of a given program were mostly below the local poverty level, but who did not recognize that their own attire, language, beliefs, values, and actions showed a dramatically different culture, would have an extremely difficult time making a good connection with the program stakeholders and building trust with them. In his chapter, Kniffley notes his repeated attention to his own culture, including elements of his own identity, that could be expected to affect how his evaluation work was received by the evaluand.

One important aspect of paying attention to culture is recognizing and taking into account the many different forms that culture takes. Some elements are enormously relevant, especially in particular settings. The cases in this book explicitly draw attention to a number of these elements, and many readers will instantly recognize the importance of most if not all of them. I suspect that as much as these resonate with readers, some of them will provide some new insights of differences and perspectives that were not familiar before encountering these cases.

Especially for evaluators, however, attending to all of these obvious cultural elements is one specific expression of the universal evaluation task of learning about the particular setting and context of the evaluand as well as attending to the many ways that the particular values, perspectives, and approaches of the evaluator interact with those details of the evaluand. Good evaluators work extensively to understand the many specifics of the program, the staff, the clients, other stakeholders, and the particular setting for all of them. Such evaluators then consider how their own values and approaches either match those of the evaluand or can be adjusted.

One element of good news is that many values and approaches do not always require either/or approaches. For example, some evaluators emphasize sophisticated inferential statistical analyses like hierarchical linear modeling or structural equation modeling. When those evaluators work with evaluands who especially value stories, unique examples, and common themes among client comments, good evaluators will make substantial efforts to find common ground like a blend of quantitative and qualitative designs. Even different analytical strategies can often be used to complement each other rather than being seen as mutually exclusive alternatives.

Styles or Forms of Cases

As noted in the Introduction section, between the time when this book was first imagined and its publication, the CASE Collaborative, a diverse group of evaluators who are committed to using Cases in evaluation teaching and learning, not only began to meet but also dove into a number of projects that include an issue of *New Directions for Evaluation* "Case-centered Teaching and Learning in Evaluation." Their working definition of a case is, "A series of events, real or imagine, that tell an evaluation story to promote student learning, including illustrating a concept, skill development, and facilitating critical thinking, among others" (Linfield & Tovey, 2021, p. 13). We use that definition in this book, and it has several implications.

First, as you will read in a number of the chapters, we include cases that have fictional elements such as using pseudonyms and changing other details to provide anonymity to real persons and organizations, combining features from several different events to make particularly useful points for learning, and simplifying or expanding descriptions of what happened to make certain elements especially clear.

Second, although the common purpose of all these cases is promoting learning about evaluation, there are a number of specific objectives that guided the particular details of individual cases. Some elements primarily illustrate aspects of evaluation such as the common experience that time, money, and other resources are in shorter supply than the evaluators and other stakeholders would prefer. Other descriptions lead to problems for the readers to solve or questions for them to answer. The details of the case provide enough information so readers understand the main elements of the specific decision presented. Still other portions provide insight into the thinking and process of decision-making by the evaluators. Readers may learn new approaches from such insights or consider under what circumstances or conditions they might make a substantially different choice. And some elements describe situations without specifying an exact problem. Readers face the additional step of determining what problems or more general questions are there to be addressed or answered. Such challenges invite reflection on what readers have already learned and can apply to new conditions.

Reflection

As noted already, cases are one especially useful strategy for students to learn many things about a particular field. They provide information about a wide range of elements. For example, cases about evaluation sometimes discuss the process of evaluators creating a logic model that illustrates the expected effects of various components of the program. Sometimes the actual logic models are included in cases. Students who may only have read about the concept of logic models can learn much more about how to create one themselves by seeing these concrete examples of this important part of an evaluation. Cases that include comments about how the evaluators thought about various aspects of the evaluation likewise provide helpful examples for students. When evaluators consider one approach but decide against it because of cost or other reasons, those new to the field can gain new insights into how to balance multiple factors.

In addition to providing information about evaluation, however, cases also offer students the opportunity to reflect on many different elements. Reading about how to create a logic model and seeing an example of one can invite the student to reflect on themselves as they consider a number of steps in the whole process. Those who have never worked on a logic model might think, "How would I take the information that the program provided here and create a logic model from it?" Those who have some experience in evaluations and logic models might think back to those occasions and think, "What did I do then that this case might suggest was a particularly good thing? What did I do then that this case might suggest could be done better, or even just differently, in the future?" Hopefully it is clear that these particular reflections are the tip of the iceberg in the many different ways that readers can think about these cases and about themselves. "How might I do something similar? How would I prefer to do something very different?"

The main point is that sometimes people get so caught up in working on a job or a larger project that they begin to focus almost exclusively on the specific task at hand and the plan they initially made for accomplishing it. Such an approach obviously has important benefits. If we do not concentrate on a limited number of items but get distracted with irrelevant details, it will be very difficult to make sustained progress. The analogy of a physical journey can be a useful one. When aiming for a particular destination, concentrating on the planned route is a very valuable approach. Paying too much attention to interesting sights off on the side has the potential to distract us from our path, and there are times when we do not have the luxury of meandering along.

But most if not all of us have had times when we thought we were following the right path, yet in fact, we had made a wrong turn or failed to make the correct turn. In such situations, continuing to do things as we have done them before, following what we think is the right path, in fact leads us further away from our goal. And making sure we are not distracted by anything other than what we are convinced is our current work may prevent us from learning that we are off course.

Reflection at least begins with a very simple step – pausing for a moment in our headlong rush to accomplish what we think is most important. The pause is essential even if it is simple, because we cannot reflect when we are intent on what we are doing. Once we pause, however, thinking about and trying to answer a few simple questions can be enormously helpful. "Is this working? Are things going the way I want them to go? Am I missing anything? Am I still on target?" This process has been called "reflection in action" (Schön, 1983; Linfield & Tovey, 2021), reflecting while in the process of doing something.

Especially while we are fully engaged in a project, it may be best to have fairly basic reflections along the lines of the questions above. If there are no signs that we are badly off course, either on a physical journey or with a particular approach to a project, there may be no obvious reason to take more than a few seconds to make sure that we do not need to make changes. Following the analogy of the physical journey, if you are driving down an interstate toward a given city, and your pause allows you to recall that you saw a sign that the city is 127 miles away, returning to the task of continuing on the interstate is a fine strategy.

But if you are on a country road, and your pause gives you the occasion to realize you have not only not seen signs for your next landmark but also you have not seen the route signs or other confirmation, you can begin to assess your situation. Returning to the main point of reflection on evaluations, a parallel insight that comes when you stop long enough to think might be that you have not heard anything from your contact at the program agency for longer than usual or something else is missing that you did not recognize when you were concentrating on a particular task.

It is probably obvious that you do not want to pause every five minutes to reflect. That would be incredibly disruptive. But having occasional brief pauses every so often may help you pick up on important opportunities more quickly. Certainly the best intervals will depend on many factors and will not be the same for everyone. Among other things, experienced evaluators begin to learn what intervals work best for them.

And it is a generally wise plan to schedule more substantial reflection times at greater intervals. For multi-year projects, including a rather sustained pause during the annual reporting cycle or a similar process may be the best approach. More substantive questions can be raised at such times – not just about minor elements, but about the project as a whole.

> Are our original goals still the best ones? Do we need any kind of shift – a small tweak to a few elements or a larger adaptation to changing circumstances? Do we need to think about additional stakeholders or others who may be involved in the program or the evaluation?

As above, these questions are samples of the kinds of reflections that may be helpful. But asking questions about major, systemic issues should happen at some point, such as annually. These times of thinking back on previous actions to consider potential changes for the future have been called "reflection on action" (Schön, 1983; Linfield & Tovey, 2021). Most of these reflections will lead to adjustments in the future, whether the near future of some next steps in the current project or the more distant future of evaluation projects that have not yet started, as opposed to changes in the next five minutes.

The Rest of the Book

Each of the cases in this book has great value on their own and present rich material for thought and learning about aspects of the actual practice of Program Evaluation that is not as obvious in more abstract presentations of the field. As such, they present a number of unique elements that complement the contributions of the other cases without duplicating them. The evaluands are different, the methods of the evaluations involve a range of approaches, and both the planned lessons and the open-ended possibilities raise many issues, questions, and directions.

Still, there are a number of important similarities among most if not all of these different cases that may be obvious to many readers, but pointing out the commonalities may be useful for others. All of the cases involve multiple stakeholders who have important differences from one another. At times, evaluators find good ways to address those differences in ways that the various stakeholders find highly satisfying. At other times, the differences create substantial conflict and there seems to be no approach that will keep everyone sufficiently happy. As students may already know, this is one of the particularly challenging aspects of evaluation.

Building on the earlier points about the cultural aspects of both the evaluand and the evaluator, these elements are almost never monolithic in any setting. For example, Kniffley notes many common experiences of abuse and maltreatment among the staff and clients that can be seen as an overall culture of the agency. But having similar experiences is not the same as having identical experiences. We encourage readers to see both large-scale similarities in culture and smaller individual differences. Among other things, evaluators often find it can be easy to miss the less obvious diversity by attending too completely to the larger similarities. We trust that readers will notice both how these cases illustrate good attention to both levels and how the subtle differences can be harder to observe.

One commonality, often expressed in some different ways, is the scarcity of resources. Time and money are some obvious areas where limitations abound in evaluation work. Evaluators often believe that they will have given amounts of each, but circumstances develop and change to reduce what is available. Another typical situation is when even conservative estimates of the number of participants turn out to be too high, and the statistical analyses that were planned to be sufficient no longer yield the levels of confidence that were expected. Even less tangible elements like participants' enthusiasm and motivation often are weaker than the various stakeholders were sure they would see.

Another way to say this is that an important lesson for readers across the cases is that unexpected and distressing developments abound in evaluation work. There almost always seem to be fewer funds, less time, fewer participants, more disagreements among key stakeholders, more changes and disruptions among the staff, and similar obstacles. Of course, although it can be easy to advise new evaluators to be prepared for unexpected developments, by definition, it is not possible to know what those unexpected changes will be. So there is no perfect way to be ready for everything. Still, these cases will illustrate many of the complications that can arise, and we encourage readers to develop a realistic sense of the kinds and range of problems that can occur.

Again, these cases provide a rich and highly useful insight into the real world and experience of evaluation. Readers will not only gain a better understanding of these elements as they read about them, conversations with classmates and discussions along the lines instructors facilitate will expand the learnings. In gathering these cases, we learned many new points and gained fresh idea. We know that each of you will also grow in your evaluation skills and knowledge from them.

References

Austin, M. J., & Packard, T. (2009). Case-based learning: Educating future human service managers. *Journal of Teaching in Social Work*, *29*(2), 216–236. https://doi.org/10.1080/08841230802240993

Elstein, A. S., Shulman, L. S., & Sprafka, S. A. (1990). Medical problem solving: A ten-year retrospective. *Evaluation and the Health Professions*, *13*(1), 5–36. https://doi.org/10.1177/016327879001300102

Jackson, J. H. (1926). The case method. *Accounting Review*, *1*(1), 108.

Kallemeyn, L. M., Bourgeois, I., & Ensminger, D. C. (2021). Editors' notes. *New Directions for Evaluation*, *2021*, 7–9.

Kawulich, B. B. (2011). Learning from action evaluation of the use of multimedia case studies in management information systems courses. *Journal of Stem Education*, *12*(7 & 8), 57–70.

Linfield, K. J., & Tovey, T. L. S. (2021). What is the case for teaching with cases in evaluation? *New Directions for Evaluation*, *2021*, 11–18. https://doi.org/10.1002/ev.20480

Montrosse-Moorhead, B., Ensminger, D. C., & Roseveare, C. (2021). How do we teach and learn with cases? *New Directions for Evaluation*, *2021*, 53–67. https://doi.org/10.1002/ev.20483

Patton, M. Q., & Patrizi, P. (2005). Case teaching and evaluation. *New Directions for Evaluation*, *2005*, 5–14. https://doi.org/10.1002/ev.141

Richardson, C. P. (1997). Using case studies in the methods classroom. *Music Educators Journal*, *84*(2), 17–22.

Schön, D. A. (1983). *The reflective practitioner: How professionals think in action*. Basic Books.

Wohlfarth, D., & Morgan, R. K. (2017). *Case studies in child and adolescent psychopathology* (2nd ed.). Waveland Press.

2 Negotiating the Complexity of Context in Evaluation

Bianca Montrosse-Moorhead and Jennie M. Weiner

Introduction

In this case, four faculty members from a flagship state university, called the University of the Northeast, are faced with a difficult decision regarding the fate of an impact evaluation of the state's Prekindergarten program they were tasked with carrying out. This evaluation was commissioned by the state's General Assembly (GA), and evaluation results have implications at the state, district, and local levels and for various stakeholders at each of these levels. How the evaluation began, the evaluation context, and the cast of characters is described first. Then, the case moves on to describing what happened in the first year of the project. In the second year, an important moment arrives – data collection is taking longer than anticipated, and a decision must be made about how to proceed. As you read through the case, consider this question: if you had been one of the faculty members involved in this evaluation, what would you do and why?

The Problem

Placing the receiver down after another long and discordant team meeting for the state Prekindergarten evaluation she was leading, Dr. Ima Soprannome let out a deep sigh. "How did we get here?" she wondered aloud. The evaluation, commissioned by the state's GA, was meant to be a boon to her and the flagship state university in which she and her team members worked. Instead, from its onset, the project was fraught with politics and difficulties that now put the team in the position of being unable to deliver the data as promised.

In response, during the past two weeks, the team came up with four potential options about how to best proceed and salvage this important work. As she read these ideas over, she couldn't help but feel anxious about what it would mean to fail or even disappoint the client. As a group of early career scholars in a state university dependent on keeping good relationships with the state legislature, educators, and schools, the stakes were high and palpable. What would their failure to deliver mean for their ability to achieve tenure? Their access to future grants and research? Their school's future funding position? It was overwhelming to think of all of what was at stake.

With the next advisory board meeting only two days away, a meeting in which the team was meant to present preliminary results, Dr. Soprannome took a steadying breath and called Dr. Tom Chadwick, the head of the Foundation for Science and Mathematics (FSM), the organization that had contracted the work for the state, to discuss the options the team had identified. She knew this call would be difficult and steeled herself for whatever lay ahead. Hopefully, one of the options would be palatable to the board and the work could proceed, if somewhat differently than originally intended.

DOI: 10.4324/9780429277788-2

The Beginning

A little over a year and a half earlier, Ima Soprannome, an assistant professor of evaluation, was sitting at her desk one cloudy winter day preparing for her evaluation class later in the week. As a second-year faculty member, she was still getting to know her colleagues, students, and the rhythms of the state university in which she worked. The campus was abuzz with faculty, staff, and students happy to be back on campus for the spring semester. Her phone rang, breaking her concentration.

Ima: Hello. Ima Soprannome.

Tom: Hello. My name is Tom Chadwick and I'm the Director of the state's Foundation for Science and Mathematics. I heard from a colleague that you specialize in evaluation. I was asked to oversee an evaluation study on behalf of our state's General Assembly. Do you think you can help me?

Ima: I'd be happy to talk to you about that. How about we start by you telling me a bit more about your needs?

Tom: Great. Well, the state's been trying to get an evaluation done of their preschool program for about 15 years now. The General Assembly finally mandated it, and actually put money behind it. About 10 years ago, they began to scope out a study like this, and hired someone to give them options. The preferred option was called a regression discontinuity study. Do you know what that is?

Ima: Yes.

Tom: Great. I'm so glad I don't have to explain it to you. It's quite complicated, as you know. Okay, well, so the design this study needs to use is set.

Ima: Okay. What are the questions you all are interested in answering?

Tom: Does preschool work? Is it a good state investment? Also, some of the people I talked to from around the state have recommended that it look at academic and non-academic outcomes.

Ima: Okay. That's helpful. A regression discontinuity could be an appropriate research methods strategy for those questions.

Tom: Great. I'm honestly not sure if it is the right design? Okay, other important details . . . let's see . . . ah yes, okay . . . we need to get a scope of work written and approved ASAP. Once approved, you all would begin recruitment right away and collect data in September. Data collection has to happen in September. And, the final report needs to be written and presented to the Education Subcommittee of the General Assembly before they break for summer during the next fiscal year so the results can be used for budget discussions.

Ima: Wow. That's a tight timeline for a study like this. Is there any flexibility?

Tom: No. We have calls to a few other evaluation experts in the state about this study. We'd love for you to do it, but if you can't do it on this timeline, and another expert can, we'll go with them.

Ima: Okay, gotcha. And, what's the budget for this study?

Tom: They have budgeted $100,000. However, you cost out what you think it will cost, and we will see what we can do.

Ima: Okay. Every project I've worked on has a range. I would hate to cost something out and it not be in the ballpark. Can you give me a sense of the range or the cap on possible funding?

Tom: It's hard to say but I think I could probably get them to go up to $150,000, but probably not any more than that. Anyway, can you do this evaluation?

Ima: Well, that's hard to say right now. It will take more than just me to carry out a study like this. I have a couple of colleagues who I think might be interested and whose expertise would be a good fit. Let me check with them, and then get back to you about setting up a face-to-face meeting.
Tom: That sounds great. But, do hurry. We haven't got much time. It's been great talking to you. I look forward to hearing from you soon.
Ima: Likewise. I'll be in touch shortly. Goodbye.

Putting down the receiver, Dr. Soprannome immediately began to put a to-do list together. While the project felt like a heavy lift on short notice, she was excited for the opportunity to build relationships in the state and do something that focused on an important issue to so many. This could open many possibilities for her and her research.

Additionally, she looked forward to inviting some of her colleagues, also early in their careers, to join her. Such work was highly valued by the university and she believed her colleagues would benefit from the chance to work on what could potentially be a high-visibility project. She knew with the right team and the state and the university behind them, this project could be a great success for all those involved.

After a few days planning her approach, Dr. Soprannome contacted several colleagues about their interest in serving on the evaluation team. She specifically sought people with expertise in early childhood education, elementary education, or educational leadership. After some initial discussions, Drs. Ruth Morris, Emily English, and Frank Mathus expressed interest in helping to co-lead this evaluation, and Dr. Soprannome set up a meeting with Dr. Chadwick for everyone to meet.

This initial meeting aimed to explore a potential collaboration between the Foundation and the University of the Northeast (UNE) to carry out the impact evaluation. After the meeting, all parties agreed to work together, and the UNE team began to craft an evaluation proposal and budget.

The Evaluation Context

As true for most state-funded and federally funded Prekindergarten programs, the state's Prekindergarten program was a means-tested (targeted) program specifically geared toward children from low-income families and low-income communities. Many of these children come from Black, Latinx, and immigrant families. Among children in these programs, 40% were Latinx, 30% were Black, 20% were White, 5% were Asian or Pacific Islander, 1% were American Indian or Native Alaskan, and 4% identified as multi-racial. Most (60%) parents or guardians had a high school diploma, and about 15% had a bachelor's degree. A quarter (25%) of parents or guardians did not finish high school. About 20% of families owned their own home.

As typical across the US personnel working in these programs did not reflect the same demographic characteristics (LoCasale-Crouch et al., 2007; Bureau of Labor Statistics at the US Department of Labor, 2015). Among Prekindergarten teachers teaching in these publicly funded programs, 80% were White, about 10% were Latinx, about 8% were Black, and the remaining 2% were a mix of American Indian or Native Alaskan, Asian or Pacific Islander, or identified as multi-racial. Almost 90% had a bachelor's degree related to early education. Because the average annual salary for Prekindergarten teachers in these programs was $31,930 per year, there was high teacher turnover. About 50% of Prekindergarten teachers owned their own home.

The program's theory of change was that it served as an early intervention strategy to improve children's readiness for kindergarten. Being more ready for kindergarten is thought to ensure children's ability to gain the knowledge, skills, attitudes, and dispositions needed to flourish in school and as adults. Some policymakers, thus, argue that the state's Prekindergarten program is part of a longer-term policy strategy for closing the state's race-based opportunity gap in childhood and beyond.

The structure of the program reflected these goals. In the state's large urban and suburban areas, approximately 60% of available seats were designated as "state-funded," while the other 40% were designated as "regular" seats for which guardians pay full tuition fees. In rural areas of the state, approximately 80% of available seats were "state-funded" while the other 20% were "regular" seats. Across the state, there were often not enough state-funded Prekindergarten seats to meet demand. All centers and schools had an application deadline, and operate on a first-come, first-serve basis, with existing families given priority consideration.

In 2014, after 15 years of implementation and use of taxpayer monies, the state's GA commissioned an evaluation of the program. Oversight for this project was given to the Education Subcommittee, a bipartisan group with members who had long supported expansion of the program across the state. Importantly, the state had been under a protracted budget crisis with officials feeling constant pressure to cut all forms of "non-essential" spending. As such, the information from the impact evaluation was meant to inform the next round of budget deliberations and could be pivotal in determining whether and how the program would continue. Members worked closely with the State Department of Education (SDE) to coordinate efforts and forward important agenda items as one voice.

With that said, at the time the study was commissioned, the SDE was in a period of transition. A new commissioner had just arrived with a long history of reform. She was eager to make her mark, especially in the area of early childhood education. At the same time, her ability to do so was impacted by the state's structure. While many educators looked to the state to provide guidance and resources, local municipalities were very powerful and many decisions about how schools operated were left to district leaders.

For example, the state guidance mandated Prekindergarten programs needed to meet eight Prekindergarten quality benchmarks as identified by the National Institute for Early Education Research (Table 2.1) and to provide six hours of programming per weekday for 180 weekdays per year. However, districts, schools, and centers had discretion about how those benchmarks were met and could choose which curriculum was used. In this way, what was

Table 2.1 National Institute for Early Education Research Program Quality Benchmarks

1. Program goals align to Early Learning and Development Standards.	5. Both teachers and assistant teachers must be required to have at least 15 hours of annual professional development.
2. A strong curriculum that is well-implemented increases support for learning and development broadly and includes specificity regarding key domains of language, literacy, mathematics, and social-emotional development.	6. Maximum class size is 20.
	7. Classes should have no more than ten children per classroom teaching staff member, that is, a staff–child ratio of 1:10.
3. Lead teachers in every classroom have at least a bachelor's degree.	8. Preschool programs ensure that children receive vision and hearing screenings and at least one additional health screening, and referrals when needed.
4. Lead teachers have specialized preparation that includes knowledge of learning, development, and pedagogy specific to preschool-age children.	

included during program hours and the structure of the program was up to the districts, schools, and centers.

To help facilitate the evaluation, the Subcommittee contracted with the "Foundation for Science and Mathematics" (FSM). The FSM was a business–community–government partnership that routinely served as an intermediary for state-commissioned studies and was completely reliant on grant or state funds for all operating costs. They have a history of getting studies done on time and within budget, and strong personal and political connections with individual legislators and high-profile community members. However, the Prekindergarten impact evaluation was the first time they worked on behalf of the Education Subcommittee. The FSM had a staff of 4: an Executive Director, a Director of Development and Operations, an Office Manager, and an Administrative Assistant.

Finally, as it too was dependent on state funding to operate, the state's flagship university, where the evaluation team worked, had faced large cuts over time. This was part of a national 30-year trend to cut state funding to institutions of higher education. Because of this, the university was constantly working with legislatures to lobby for the university and funding for its operating costs. It also pushed faculty to find ways to work with the legislature and other government bodies to highlight the university's function in providing value for the state and its larger needs (e.g., education, workforce development, industry). In this context, faculty members, most often White and from middle-class and upper-class backgrounds, were often tasked with evaluating programs aimed at addressing the needs of many of the state's more vulnerable and traditionally marginalized communities – often those who identified as People of Color and/or poor. Few faculty shared the same lived experiences as the participants. It was into these conditions the members of the evaluation team were hired and began their work with FSM.

Evaluation Planning Begins

Right after the evaluation contract was awarded, the Provost called Dr. Soprannome to congratulate her and the team,

> You know, it's great for us to be able to work with our state colleagues on behalf of children and families in the state. I and everyone here at UNE are so excited you were asked to lead this effort. Someone from our university press office will be calling you all. We'd like to promote this work across the state to show how we are giving back. Plus, it will help us make the case for all that we do for the state when we go into the next round of budget talks.

Shortly after the Provost's call, the UNE faculty team was invited to FSM to meet with Dr. Chadwick and the Senate Education Subcommittee chairperson, Manny Reed. At the meeting, it was made clear that Dr. Chadwick would serve as the point-person for Subcommittee, field their questions and keep them abreast of how the evaluation was progressing. He said,

> My biggest concern is that this study gets done, done well, and that it is free from any political influence. I have a reputation to uphold, as I oversee lots of studies for the General Assembly. They know they can trust me.

Senator Reed also spoke, highlighting the Subcommittee's commitment to Prekindergarten education in the state and enthusiasm regarding the study and its results.

I'm very proud of the early childhood work we have done in the state. I constantly sing the praises of our early childhood educators who are doing a fantastic job. I know the program works, and this evaluation needs to show that.

Though the team had just begun to plan the evaluation, it was clear that many in the state had already heard it was happening and had strong views about the approach. For example, the Commissioner of Education and school district personnel made their feelings regarding the evaluation known early on, calling the school of education's Dean to express their concerns. As the Dean conveyed to the team as he called them into his office during the earlier planning stages of the evaluation, one of the district superintendents said,

You should know that I'm also hearing that many early childhood schools and centers are nervous, and that's not just in our district, but across districts. They are all working hard, and are nervous that the results will not confirm that. Also, they are nervous about the proposed design. They are worried and a bit uncomfortable about losing valuable class time for an evaluation that may not even best represent the high quality of their work.

Given the interest in this evaluation and its size, the evaluation team put together a study advisory committee. Representatives from the state and school districts were invited to serve, in addition to experts in quantitative research methods, evaluation, and early childhood education. As the study advisory committee was being assembled, one faculty member with expertise in quantitative methods said,

I'm so excited I was asked to join this committee and am relieved to hear an RDD method was mandated. That is considered best practice in terms of causal inference, and I see my role as adding some 'gravitas' to the study and making sure you all get it right.

While perhaps a bit less explicit, the other three members with similar expertise conveyed similar sentiments (e.g., "Happy to support you with my expertise," "Glad to use my expertise to ensure another well executed study").

The two faculty members with expertise in early childhood education also saw their role as safeguarding the integrity of such programs and their impact. As one such member explained,

You know, I've seen lots of prek impact studies that use an RDD approach. Not all of them are done well. I'm really concerned about the assessments that seem to be the norm in these types of studies, as they routinely focus on a discrete skill, for example, can kids recognize letters, words, or numbers. Rarely do they focus on all aspects of early language and mathematics development. None focus on the other parts of the prek curriculum standards.

Finally, the representatives on the board from the state's department of education and its early childhood office were supportive of the study as they saw it as a lever to ensure future investments. As one of them said,

I cannot wait for this evaluation to show how good this program is. We have been wanting to expand our state-funded prekindergarten program for years, and this may be the thing that helps us do that. How can I help you get this done?

However, the four representatives from some of the state's school districts were the least enthusiastic to participate. They were highly suspect of any initiatives or evaluations originating from the state or the university, which they considered a state actor. As one of them said, "My job is to represent the interests of our urban and rural districts. I'm not sure their interests and the state's study align."

A description of the entire cast of characters in this evaluation is included in Appendix A.

The Evaluation Process: Early Decisions and Actions

As the proposal and budget were being developed, Dr. Soprannome and Dr. Chadwick met one-on-one with several high-level individuals to ascertain what they believed the evaluation needed to focus on, identify potential barriers and gatekeepers, and get preliminary feedback on the proposed evaluation design. These individuals included Senator Manny Reed, the State Commissioner of Education, the Division Directors of the State Department of Education's Early Childhood Division and the Data Warehouse Division, a few key District Superintendents, and the Directors of Research and Evaluation in large urban school districts. It was clear from these early meetings and the aforementioned phone calls to the Dean that there was mixed support for the study. The two largest concerns were that the evaluation would find no or negative effects putting the entire system in jeopardy, and the research design which, despite the state mandating its use, few, beyond those with deep evaluation expertise, seemed to understand.

To be clear, the fears associated with programmatic performance were grounded in the evaluation rather than the success of Prekindergarten in the state. Everyone involved in these higher-level discussions was positive it was working. However, not everyone believed the study would be able to detect that success. Comments like "There are so many variables that play a role in what happens in Prekindergarten, and how are you going to take those into account?" were common. Others had doubts that an RDD design was appropriate in this context. For example, one district Director of Research and Evaluation said,

> I learned about regression discontinuity studies in graduate school, and I know that they require a lot, like way more data than other types of studies, to be able to pick up an effect, if there is one. You all are going to need to be thoughtful about how you are going to get a sample that large and one that generalizes to the state as a whole. You know that districts, centers, and schools are not required to participate in evaluation studies commissioned by the state, right?

In response to such questions, the team would repeat the Senate's charge that they use an RDD design, point to other well-regarded research that used RDD to evaluate prekindergarten programs elsewhere, and to resources including those they created to explain how an RDD facilitates causal inferencing. (An abbreviated description of a regression discontinuity design is included in Appendix B.) And yet, despite all these efforts, such questions often asked repeatedly by the same individuals persisted.

Due to the number of people consulted and what seemed to be some hesitancy among the various stakeholder groups to begin, it took longer than anticipated to get initial approvals for the budget and approach. During this time, it became clear that beginning to collect data in September was not possible, and the best course of action was to move the study to the following academic year. This change also meant that the $150,000 originally budgeted for the evaluation would not be enough to complete it on the extended timeline. After several rounds of negotiation, an evaluation plan was approved that focused on examining the average effect of attending a state-funded Prekindergarten program on children's early language and mathematics skills. The evaluation team had wanted to also examine behavior, a core component of the state's Prekindergarten curriculum, but there was not enough money to do so. A power analysis suggested that data would need to be collected from a random sample of 1,250 children equally split between the treatment and comparison conditions, so the team budgeted for 1,600 children to account for anticipated attrition. Given their prior positive experiences with study recruitment and the state's willingness to reach out to prek sites directly to encourage participation, the team assumed that nearly all those identified for the study would participate. The total budget was $250,000 across two years.

The Evaluation Process: Year 1

Since the evaluation team now had a year before data collection would commence, they planned to spend the first year gaining Internal Review Board (IRB) approval for the study (a required step for most research, particularly if the results were to be published), putting the study advisory committee together, and planning for data collection in the fall of year 2. Team members were relieved and felt confident that they would be ready to engage when the next school year began. Given all the concerns about the project, a stakeholder engagement plan was also developed and implemented so the team could be in dialogue with various stakeholders to continue to understand the nature of concerns, work to address those concerns, and hopefully facilitate buy-in and cooperation at the state, district, and local levels.

The evaluation team was insistent on getting the IRB approval for three reasons. One, they had negotiated approval with the state to disseminate study results to the academic community via conference presentations and journal manuscripts; a necessary output for early career tenure-track faculty. Two, given the politics surrounding the evaluation, the IRB was one mechanism to protect the independence of the evaluation team. Three, given the nature of the data and specifically that they would be collecting student-level information, they wanted independent verification that their plans for protecting human subjects were sound.

The IRB approval process took 6 months. Much of the data the study team needed from the state and districts (e.g., class rosters) or to collect fell under both federal human protection regulations and the Family Educational Rights and Privacy Act (FERPA). Negotiating the protection of data was a relatively smooth process. What took longer however was negotiating whether consent would be opt-in or opt-out. Normally, consent processes are opt-in, meaning that human subjects (i.e., participants and/or their guardians) must state that they wish to participate in the study – in this case the parents of Prekindergarten and kindergarten students. However, existing research showed that in several Prekindergarten impact evaluations carried out in other states, those that took an opt-in strategy had significantly lower response rates than those with an opt-out strategy. In other words, when given the option, the research showed that parents tended not to actively pursue evaluation participation, but did not refuse either. The evaluation team was able to use this research to show that the risk–benefit ratio was worse in opt-in studies. It took a few months for the IRB and the evaluation team to come to agreement about the opt-out process (e.g., how long parents and students would have to decide, by what means). The lag time with the IRB approval meant that the study team could not reach out to, or communicate with, schools and centers, and through them, parents and other caregivers, until halfway through the first year.

The study advisory committee was also important in those early days of the study. They met and provided feedback on the initial plan, and the revised plan when data collection was postponed until year 2. Once the two-year evaluation plan was approved, the advisory board was to be called together at key points during the evaluation process to provide feedback and support.

After the IRB approval came, the evaluation team began to implement their stakeholder engagement plan. Although the evaluation team wanted to personally visit schools and centers to meet and explain the study and its purposes, it was infeasible. There were 75 Prekindergarten schools and centers spread across 32 districts. The comparison group involved collecting data from kindergarten sites, which involved 313 schools. They could communicate directly with the school districts and they asked each district to identify a point-person with whom they would meet and work. The team met one-on-one with each district representative, sometimes more than once, to discuss the study. Often representatives would talk about the concerns they were hearing from other colleagues at the district office, or from the centers and schools they served. It was not uncommon to hear things like, "I know we've been through this before, but there are still concerns about this study." The evaluation team did their best to try to address concerns including continuing to emphasize that the evaluation would look at the average effect and that no one school would be identified, named, or called out; continuing to describe the study design in clear non-technical terms, and often involving visuals; explaining who would have access to the data and who would not; and explaining why the study had been commissioned in the first place. In addition, the evaluation team asked the Commissioner of Education to write a letter of support for the study, and this letter was circulated to distinct offices, elementary schools, and Prekindergarten sites. The evaluation team also prepared a one-page, front and back, teacher-friendly flier about the study that identified the concerns they were hearing, provided responses from the evaluation team, and included contact information for Dr. Soprannome in case they had additional questions or concerns (see Appendix C), and asked each district point-person to circulate it to schools and centers. Going into the summer before data collection was to begin, relationships were established and the evaluation team felt they had good rapport with most, but not all, of the district point-persons. It was also unclear how much buy-in for the study they were able to cultivate, particularly among schools and centers (i.e., the groups most closely connected with parents and caregivers).

On this note, the evaluation team also discussed how to communicate with parents and legal guardians about the study. The decision was made to ask the school and center staff to be the point-person for teachers. The assumption was that staff and parents and guardians had positive and trusting relationships, and because staff interacted with parents and guardians daily, it would be better for them to explain the study's purpose, thus putting parents' minds at ease regarding participation. Moreover, because school staff are often the point of contact for parents who wish to opt their child out of participating in standardized testing, the study team assumed parents would also feel comfortable telling school staff if they wished to opt out of the study. Also, truth be told, as the evaluation team did not anticipate that parents would have strong objections to the study, this was the least articulated element of the stakeholder engagement plan. Their previous experiences with such requests were that parents gave little pushback to mandates coming down from the state or district offices.

The Evaluation Process: A Critical Decision Point Happens in Year 2

The team required both the state's Prekindergarten and kindergarten class rosters to conduct the evaluation. Year 2 rosters for Prekindergarten programs were sent to the study team in June; however, the class rosters for kindergarten were not sent until early September. The state department had appointed a data liaison who agreed to pull the data, but the work for the evaluation was not deemed a priority and so the liaison continued to preference several other data requests, creating the delay. This meant that the team needed to move more quickly than anticipated to identify a random sample of kindergarten students who had attended a state-funded Prekindergarten the previous academic year (comparison group).

The notification process for both Prekindergarten and kindergarten sites looked the same. Once students were randomly selected, the center directors and school principals were notified via e-mail how many students were randomly selected for testing. Per the approved IRB, sites had a two-week period to opt out as did parents of students who were selected. The sites were responsible for notifying parents and relaying this information to them, which was the same process used for the state's annual testing program.

When members of the study team began to reach out to principals and directors to set up a time to do the student testing, it was clear there were problems. Some of the principals and directors did not receive the e-mail, which was easily remedied, but it also meant the two-week opt-out window had to start anew. Others refused to return phone calls of study team members. And still others opted their district out entirely, bringing the total number of students down to 1,300 before data collection even began. Moreover, the team was also fielding a number of calls from the district point-people with complaints from centers and sites about the study. These complaints mirrored exactly those the evaluation team members had dealt with during year 1 and had worked hard to address. As a result, team members spent far more of their time than budgeted helping to address these concerns, coordinate the study, contact schools, contact district point-people, and/or collect data.

While team members were willing to do what was needed, the extra time had begun to cut into their ability to fully fulfill their other university-based work responsibilities (i.e., other research, teaching, and service). While they hadn't heard complaints from colleagues per se about the shift in their time use, the Dean had started sometimes "dropping in" on some of their team meetings when they used the glass conference room on the third floor near his office. Saying that he "just wanted to hear what's up" or that he was "here if you need me," team members sensed he was worried and wanted to make sure they knew they were being watched and were expected to perform.

The original evaluation timeline had data collection wrapping up in November, and as time progressed, it was clear this evaluation milestone would not be met. By early November, data had only been collected from 400 students, 225 from the treatment group, and 175 from the comparison group. This number was significantly below the 1,250 students the team needed for the study to be able to detect an effect, if there was one.

Moreover, the evaluation team's relationship with Dr. Chadwick was rapidly deteriorating. Frustrated at the lack of progress, Dr. Chadwick had begun to send messages that he viewed the team as responsible for the issues they were facing and believed they were not acting forcefully enough to rectify the situation. Saying he wanted to be able to keep closer track of their efforts so he could answer the Senate Subcommittee's or other questions and concerns, Dr. Chadwick had demanded the evaluation team send weekly response rate updates via e-mail. Rather than assuage concern or help with communication however, these reports appeared to only make Dr. Chadwick feel more negatively about the team's efforts. Thus, it was perhaps no surprise that when he and Dr. Soprannome met in person in early November to discuss the project and their collective concerns, the tone quickly turned acrimonious.

Tom: Look, I really don't understand why the data is coming in so slowly. We need it now.
Ima: We are working as hard as we can. As you know, we did a lot of things last year to try to lay the groundwork for a smooth data collection process. We also worked quickly

	to identify the kindergarten sample, even though that data came in 3 months late. We have to give sites and centers a 2 week opt out period, and for half of the sites, that turned into a month-long process because they said that they didn't receive the email. The biggest problems we are facing are opt outs from centers and schools and parents and guardians and non-response. The opt out we cannot do anything about, as we cannot make centers, sites, teachers, and students participate in this study. We are getting a lot of angry calls from parents and guardians, by the way, about this study. I've also heard that districts, centers, and schools are also getting a lot of calls from parents. That said, we are working with the district point-person to try to reach directors and principals that are non-responsive, as we do not have the capacity to visit those centers ourselves.
Tom:	My reputation is for getting things done. This is hurting my reputation and that of the foundation. Can you just give me the list of non-responders and I'll use my connections to make sure they respond?
Ima:	No, that would violate our approved IRB. I cannot violate the confidentiality of participants even if they are non-responders.
Tom:	Fine. This is BS by the way, and I think you would feel differently if it was your neck on the line. I'm calling an emergency study advisory committee meeting for next week. We need to let them know what is going on. You and your team need to come up with possible scenarios for moving forward. I hope you have a good plan as Senator Reed is going to be none too pleased to hear this.
Ima:	Next week?!? How about two weeks to give us enough time to come up with viable, thoughtful options? Plus, it might be hard for the advisory committee to come together in 1 week, and I think we probably want as many perspectives on all this as possible.
Tom:	Fine, two weeks it is. But these plans better be worth the week wait.

The study team worked hard over the two weeks to prepare for the study committee meeting and develop workable options. They came up with four options:

1. Call it: This scenario would require the evaluation team to continue to collect as much data as possible through the end of November. They would need to develop a new data analysis plan, with feedback from the advisory committee, to account for the response rate. The rest of the evaluation timeline would remain the same, meaning the spring semester would be devoted to data cleaning, data analysis, and report writing so that everything could be done in time for the May and the state budget negotiations.
2. Adjust the Year 2 data collection timeline: This scenario would require the evaluation team to extend data collection into the spring semester, and significantly ramp up outreach to schools and centers by calling them every other day until a response was received (opt out or set a date/time for data collection). This would significantly truncate the time available for cleaning and analyzing the data, and writing the report so that it could be ready in time for the next round of budget negotiations in May.
3. Pivot and treat Year 2 as a pilot: This scenario would require that the evaluation team spend the rest of Year 2 continuing to build good will with the centers and schools, and the team would need to develop a new plan for this purpose. The state would have to extend the contract to Year 3, and it would require another $100,000 in funding. This additional funding would be used to purchase additional testing materials, and pay faculty salaries, graduate student stipends, and data collector wages.

4. Other: The evaluation team wanted to leave open the possibility that there was a potential fourth option, and so left an "other" option on the table.

The team presented these options at the advisory board meeting. After an hour of tough questioning, some which seemed to imply the team had not done their best to ensure full participation during this round of collection, no consensus could be reached. The experts and stakeholder representatives were about evenly split across the three options. None offered an alternative option. In the end, the advisory board put the decision back on the evaluation team. The evaluation team was advised to pick a decision, document it, including why it was selected over the alternatives, and move forward. The evaluation team had to make a decision.

What Would You Do?

Consider all of the information contained in the case. If you were a PI or Co-PI on this evaluation, which option would you choose? What are your reasons for selecting this option?

Disclaimer

This case was inspired by an evaluation Drs. Montrosse-Moorhead and Weiner conducted. The actual details of the case were culled from several program evaluations we carried out individually and collectively, and are not necessarily representative of the "true experience" of any particular evaluation. This is a work of fiction on which the "facts" are based on real experiences we have encountered across our work, and our interpretation of those experiences. In other words, yes, these things really happened. No, they did not all happen in the same evaluation, although they could have.

Appendix A
Cast of Characters for the State-Funded Prekindergarten Program Evaluation

Table 2.2 Cast of Characters

Name, Title	Background, Concerns, and Issues
Evaluation Role: Impact evaluation study	
Dr. Ima Soprannome, Primary Investigator	Dr. Soprannome received her doctorate in evaluation and research methodology, where she specialized in educational evaluation. She was new to the state, as she recently joined UNE as an assistant professor of evaluation. She has already led several large-scale evaluations.
Dr. Ruth Morris, Co-Primary Investigator)	Dr. Morris received her doctorate in educational leadership. Her research re-frames educational leadership and change to make both more inclusive, equitable, and oriented toward collective uplift and continuous improvement. She was a middle and high school history teacher. She was new to the state and UNE, where she recently started as Assistant Professor of Educational Leadership.
Dr. Emma English, Co-Primary Investigator	Dr. English received her doctorate in education, with an emphasis on early childhood literacy. Before earning her doctorate, she was an elementary school teacher and principal. She grew up in the state and was now Assistant Professor of Curriculum and Instruction.
Dr. Frank Mathus, Co-Primary Investigator	Dr. Mathus received his doctorate in education, with an emphasis on mathematics education. Before earning his doctorate, he taught middle school mathematics. He was new to UNE, but not to the state, and serves as Assistant Professor of Curriculum and Instruction.
Graduate Students	The evaluation contract provided funding for four graduate students to join the team. One was pursuing a doctorate in evaluation; a second a doctorate in educational leadership. The other two were pursuing doctorates in curriculum and instruction. All were former elementary school teachers.
Team of data collectors	A team of 60 data collectors were hired and trained to administer the norm-referenced instruments to Prekindergarten and kindergarten students in the evaluation. They were recruited from UNE and were undergraduate students majoring in education.
Evaluation Role: Primary Stakeholders	
Dr. Tom Chadwick, Executive Director of the state's Foundation for Science and Mathematics	The General Assembly asked Dr. Tom Chadwick to put together an evaluation team and serve as an intermediary and fiscal agent between the Education Subcommittee and the evaluation team. He holds a doctorate in biology, and built a career in industry (research and development), working his way up the leadership ladder, prior to joining the Foundation as its ED.
Senator Manny Reed, Chair of the Education Subcommittee	Senator Reed has long supported early childhood education in the state. He, along with other members of the Education Subcommittee, was very interested in study results. Some wanted to see an expansion of Prekindergarten programming, and others wanted to understand if Prekindergarten funding had been a good investment of state funds.

Name, Title	Background, Concerns, and Issues
Evaluation Role: Other Stakeholders	
State Education Department [SED] leaders	The Commissioner and employees working in the early education division provided early learning standards, guidance, and funding to local school districts. They also oversaw state licensing of early childhood schools and centers.
School district personnel	District staff helped early childhood schools and centers interpret learning standards and guidance, and disperse funds to centers and schools. They also served as an intermediary between the state department of education and the early childhood schools and centers.
Early childhood schools and centers	Personnel working for each early childhood school and center were on the ground implementers of the state-funded Prekindergarten program. Using the standards and guidance provided by the state and with assistance from the school district office, each school, or center developed and implemented a plan for their Prekindergarten program.
University of the Northeast (UNE), State flagship university	The university, for which the evaluation team members worked, received approximately half of its annual budget from the state. Every time a new budget was developed, the university had to lobby the state for funding.
Study advisory committee	This committee was composed of methodological and educational experts and state department and school district representatives who served as a sounding board for and advisers of the evaluation team. Four members had expertise in quantitative research methods and two in early childhood education, and all were from different universities in the northeast. There was also a representative from the state department of education, and the early childhood office within the department. There were four representatives from the school districts. These representatives were nominated by the districts themselves, and included a mix of urban and rural districts. No teachers, parents, students, or Prekindergarten principals or directors were asked to join the advisory board.
Parents and guardians of children randomly selected for inclusion in the study	Because the program was directed at serving Black, Latinx, immigrant, and low-income families, many of the children and families served reflected these demographics. Due to their own schooling experiences, and/or other negative interactions with bureaucratic and often discriminatory systems, some of the parents and guardians of children attending early childhood schools and centers in the study did not automatically view school positively. For good reason, they did not automatically trust school personnel, who often did not share parent's and/ or guardians' backgrounds or experiences, to always "do the right thing" in terms of acting in the best interest of their child. Moreover, for many, the choice to send their children to Prekindergarten was not a choice at all. Many had to work, they had no other support system to take the place of Prekindergarten or could not afford an alternative school to the one state provided, and so they had no choice but to send their children to these schools and centers.

Appendix B
Abbreviated Description of a Regression Discontinuity Design

Despite the name not being very friendly to non-methodologists, regression discontinuity designs (labeled "RD" hereafter) is a useful quasi-experimental method for determining whether, on average, a program or treatment is effective. This design is particularly useful when, for example, ethical reasons prevent you from using a lottery or random assignment process. This is the case in prekindergarten programs. It would be unethical for anyone to randomly decide which kids get to go to prekindergarten and which do not.

In an RD design, we *cannot* create two groups for comparison from kindergarten (K) kids only, because the kids who show up in kindergarten, but did not go to state-funded prekindergarten, do not meet the first condition for comparison. That is, they *never planned to attend* this type of prekindergarten program. This creates potential differences that could skew or bias results. For example, Orfilia is a new immigrant and so wasn't in the state. Christian went to an excellent private prekindergarten. Tran stayed home with her grandmother (see Picture 2.1).

We can, however, create two comparison groups using kids who go to state-funded prekindergarten, using information about (a) their birthdays and (b) enrollment cutoff date (3 or 4 years old on or by September 1 in most states). In this scenario, whether you were born on a day that made you eligible for PreK is random, and naturally creates control and treatment groups. For example, there is really little difference between a child born on August 31 and September 2. But, the child born on August 31 can start prekindergarten when they are 4 years old, but the child born on September 2 must wait until the next year. For kids close to the enrollment eligibility date (September 1), the only difference between these two groups is that one group can complete prekindergarten and the other has to wait until the next year. So, we can compare where these two children are a year later, where the child born on August 31 completed prekindergarten and serves as the "treatment" group. And the child born on September 2 did not complete prekindergarten the previous year and is starting prekindergarten this year, and serves as the "comparison" or "control" group.

For an RD to be appropriate, a few key features must be present. One, there must be some sort of cutoff. In this case, it is a combination of a child's birthdate, age, and enrollment

Kids in K who **planned to attend** state-funded PreK

Kids in K who **did not plan to attend** state-funded PreK

Picture 2.1 Non-equivalent groups of children

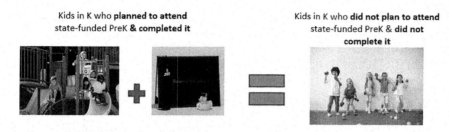

Picture 2.2 Equivalent groups of children

cutoff date. Two, the cutoff must be based on a cut-off value on a continuous quantitative pre-program measure. Three, the cutoff must not be able to be manipulated. This means that all persons on one side of the cutoff are assigned to one group, and all persons on the other side of the cutoff are assigned to the other group. (See Picture 2.2.)

Also, for the analysis, one typically looks at kids who fall within "windows of eligibility." For example, only analyzing kids whose birthdays fall within +/-1 month of the enrollment cutoff date, within +/-3 months, etc. If the pattern of results is the same across all of those "windows of eligibility," then we have strong evidence of whatever result is identified.

For you to be able to analyze different "windows of eligibility," an RD requires sometimes as much as 2.75 times the participants as a randomized experiment. For instance, if a randomized experiment needs 100 participants to achieve a certain level of power, the RD design might need as many as 275. This is because you need enough participants on both sides of the cutoff to be able to detect an effect if there is one. Moreover, you want to keep your data collection windows as tight as possible to the cutoff, ideally within 3 months of the cutoff, to be able to make the strongest argument possible about effects.

For a more technical description of RD studies, we refer readers to two free resources:

1. Trochim's (2020, March) description in the *Research Methods Knowledge Base* (https://conjointly.com/kb/regression-discontinuity-design/).
2. Jacob, Zue, Somers, and Bloom's (2012, July) *A Practical Guide to Regression Discontinuity* (www.mdrc.org/sites/default/files/regression_discontinuity_full.pdf).

Appendix C
Teacher-Friendly Flier About the State-Funded Prekindergarten Program Evaluation

Frequently Asked Questions About the Prek Evaluation

What is a regression discontinuity study? Why is the state doing this type of study? An independent consultant identified the regression discontinuity (RD) approach as the best approach to understand the *average* impact of state-funded prekindergarten. This design was recommended given that random assignment of children to PreK attendance would not be feasible and is unethical. An RD approach is considered the best practice in PreK impact evaluations. The evaluation will collect data from two groups of students, compare their outcomes, and determine, on average, do children who attend state-funded prekindergarten have higher early language and mathematics skills. Visually, the two groups of children are seen in Figure 2.1:

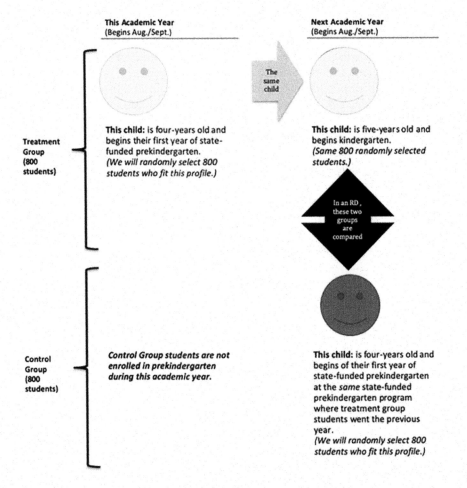

Figure 2.1 Visual showing the two groups of children for analysis

Table 2.3 Students Eligible for Study

Prekindergarten Students	Kindergarten Students
• Four-year-old students at the beginning of their first year of state-sponsored prekindergarten. • Students in head start prekindergarten programs will *not* be included in the study.	• Only kindergarten students that attended state-sponsored prekindergarten the previous year. • Only kindergarten students that attended state-sponsored prekindergarten for 1 year.

Which students are eligible for inclusion? *Table 2.3 shows which students are eligible to be included in the study.*

Does my school/center need to participate? There is currently no legislation that requires participation. The state's General Assembly requested this study because of its need for credible information that provides an indication as to the benefit to children participating in state-funded prekindergarten. For this reason, we hope you will participate.

Will parents/legal guardians have the option to opt out of having their child be part of the assessment if their child is randomly selected? Yes, per our approved child protection process, parents or legal guardians will have the option to opt out of having their child be part of the evaluation. The evaluation team will provide a parent/legal guardian opt out letter for each child that is randomly selected.

What will be required of my school/center if one of our kids is randomly selected to participate? If one or more children from your school/center is randomly selected, you will be asked to identify ONE person at your school/center to serve as a point-of-contact during the data collection process. Duties include: communicating with the evaluation team to coordinate data collection days and times; sending the parent/legal guardian opt out letter home at least 2 weeks before we collect data; locating adults to observe administration of the assessment, and ensuring the adults are present during data collection days and times; and helping the evaluation team locate the randomly chosen kindergarten and prekindergarten students.

What assessments materials will be used in this study? Consistent with the best practice in PreK impact evaluations, we will use standardized tests, specifically the *Woodcock-Johnson*, to measure students' emergent reading skills, oral expression, and mathematics skills. This test was selected because it has been used in Prekindergarten impact evaluations in at least ten states, they provide for a more complete understanding of early language and mathematics skills (as opposed to focusing on a discrete skill like letter or number recognition), and have been shown to be reliable and provide valid scores, especially when given by a trained assessor.

How much time will it take to test each child? It will take approximately 45–50 minutes per child.

How often will each child be tested? Each child will only need to be tested once.

How will the results of the study be reported? The evaluation team will write a report of findings, and it will be made available to the General Assembly and its' Education Subcommittee, the State Department of Education, Superintendents, and schools and centers. Please know that results will *not* be reported at the district, town, school, or prekindergarten program level. Results will be aggregated and reported at the state level. No one will be able to determine which sites and students were sampled for this study. In other words, there will be no way for anyone to link information back to your students, teachers, school, town, or district.

What if I have other questions? Please contact Ima Soprannome at ima@une.edu or 888.888.1234.

References

LoCasale-Crouch, J., Konold, T., Pianta, R., Howes, C., Burchinal, M., Bryant, D., Clifford, R., Early, D., & Barbarin, O. (2007). Observed classroom quality profiles in state-funded pre-kindergarten programs and associations with teacher, program, and classroom characteristics. *Early Childhood Research Quarterly, 22*(1), 3–17. https://doi.org/10.1016/j.ecresq.2006.05.001

Bureau of Labor Statistics at the US Department of Labor. (2015, May). *Sector 61: Educational services (including private, state, and local government schools)*. Retrieved from https://www.bls.gov/oes/special.requests/oes_research_2015_sec_61.xlsx

3 Professional and Interpersonal Competencies in an Evaluation Capacity Building Collective Impact Project

Leanne Kallemeyn and Jay Wade

Introduction

This case engages professional competencies and ethical issues when using an evaluation capacity building approach with a community-based organization. This case also exemplifies culturally responsive evaluation, a stance that is relevant in all evaluation contexts. In this chapter, we set the stage for the focus of this case on professional and interpersonal competencies, evaluation capacity building, and culturally responsive evaluation. We then introduce you to the actors in our case, providing background on the evaluand and context. Our play unfolds through five acts representing different aspects of an evaluation process – focusing the evaluation, building relationships, methods and strategies, findings, and reporting. Each act includes an interlude with discussion questions. Be prepared for increasing audience participation (that's you the reader) with each act. Finally, we conclude with a postscript in which we each provide our reflections and responses to the case.

Setting the Stage: Competencies, Evaluation Capacity Building, and Culturally Responsive Evaluation

In 2018, the American Evaluation Association (AEA) released new competencies to guide evaluator practice in five domains: professional practice, methodology, context, planning and management, and interpersonal. Although competencies in all five domains are critical, this case highlights competencies in two domains – professional practice (domain 1) and interpersonal (domain 5).

Evaluation capacity building (ECB) refers to "the intentional work to continuously create and sustain overall organizational processes that make quality evaluation and its uses routine" (Compton et al., 2002a, p. 14). In recent decades, ECB has grown substantially. Although there are some cases that exemplify what ECB is (Compton et al., 2002b; King, 2002; Taut, 2007; Nielsen et al., 2011; Hilton & Libretto, 2017), there are minimal, open-ended cases to address the ethical dilemmas that evaluators encounter. Although this case is based in a US context, international development projects are increasingly utilizing ECB; thus, it may have applicability to wide audiences (Valéry & Shakir, 2005; Tarsilla, 2014).

Culturally responsive evaluators recognize power and privilege embedded within culture, and ensure their evaluations and discourses are used to address marginalization and oppression rather than promote it (Hood et al., 2015). Consequently, evaluation involves including stakeholders from the cultural contexts of a particular program or policy in all phases of an evaluation and having members of an evaluation team that represent the cultures affiliated with a project. Evaluators ensure that the questions asked, approaches to data collection

DOI: 10.4324/9780429277788-3

and analysis used, and how findings are shared align with the cultural values and beliefs of program participants. Scholars assert that understanding culture and context are critical in all evaluation approaches; thus, culturally responsive evaluation complements other approaches rather than being a distinct approach (Hood et al., 2014). The American Evaluation Association (AEA, 2011) statement on Cultural Competence outlines essential practices, including acknowledging the complexity of cultural identity, recognizing the dynamics of power, recognizing and eliminating biases in language, and employing culturally appropriate methods.

In ECB the role of the evaluator shifts to being a coach (Ensminger et al., 2015; Wade et al., 2016), and thus introduces distinct ethical challenges. The evaluator is teaching and supporting stakeholders in carrying out their own evaluation. The stakeholders ultimately have responsibility for carrying out and using the evaluation. The role of the evaluator in culturally responsive evaluation may be an activist stance toward evaluation with explicit work for social justice (Neubauer et al., 2020).

In these roles, evaluators encounter several ethical challenges. What if the stakeholders do not practice or value systematic inquiry, despite extensive efforts to educate, model, and provide support? What if the stakeholders are not doing so with integrity? What if the stakeholders are looking out for their own well-being or their own organization rather than social justice? What if the evaluator questions the competence of a stakeholder for carrying out evaluation in an organization? How does an evaluator lead such a process when an outsider to the community? How does an evaluator lead a culturally responsive process that addresses power imbalances to promote the good of the community? This case provides real-world contexts to grapple with these ethical questions. Although the case itself is fictitious, it is rooted in the authors' experiences from multiple evaluation projects.

Meet the Actors: Description of the Evaluand and Context[1]

EvalCapacity is a non-profit organization that provides services in strategic planning and evaluation capacity building to other non-profit organizations. They have three full-time staff members – Victoria VanDyke, who is a White woman who founded and continues to lead the organization, Kontrell Miles, an African American man who is a data analyst, and Emily McDonnell, a White woman who provides evaluation project management across projects. The organization also has six part-time staff members. They are a diverse organization with over 50% staff of color; however, only one of the three leaders of the organization is a person of color. None of the staff are from the neighborhood being served in this project. Over the last ten years, they have built strong partnerships with several community organizations and local foundations.

Recently, a program officer from the Community Education Foundation, Ms. Keesha Turner, who identifies as African American and whom they had partnered with on several initiatives, reached out regarding partnering to provide capacity building support for their initiative, Summer Kummunity for Youth (SKY). SKY was a collective impact project that was building a network between education, health, and social service organizations that support youths, K-6, during the summer in a historically underserved neighborhood in a large, urban city. In the past, many of the organizations involved depended on volunteers and had limited experience with evaluating their programming. Due to the innovative program model and strong anecdotal reports of impact, the foundation had supported the program for the past two years, which allowed the program to move from volunteer efforts to paid staff. For the past two years, however, outcomes continued to be anecdotal – the Foundation's Board wanted to see more specific outcomes and support the organization's capacity to do evaluation in the future. As a result, they hired EvalCapacity to do ECB work with the program and support them through an outcomes-focused evaluation effort.

The neighborhood, in previous decades, had several factories that provided employment opportunities, but as the factories closed the residents of the neighborhood moved to find work or remained in the area with minimal employment opportunities. Redlining was a common experience in the community. Local and state authorities continually chose not to invest resources to rebuild the community; instead, the neighborhood nearby received extensive capital investments that attracted start-up technology companies. Due to this economic divide, within a couple of decades, a divide in the resources and quality of the local schools, parks, and other community resources was evident. Most residents were African American families that had homes and roots in the neighborhood and were committed to its revitalization.

Dr. Cassandra Mack was born and raised in the community. She attended a historically Black college a few hours away, and eventually a graduate program in social work. After graduating, she was called back to serve her neighborhood. She started as a school social worker, and early in her career developed several after-school initiatives for youth. Eventually, she formed a non-profit, FutureNetwork, to sustain and grow the activities. She aimed to inspire and support students to attend college, as she had done.

Dr. Mack seemed happy to accept the ECB effort, as were the staff, who were excited to document their impact. The project began with a focus on evaluation of the program through building the capacity of program partners to identify, measure, and report their outcomes; however, as EvalCapacity embedded itself in FutureNetwork, organizational, and programmatic issues emerged, which impacted relationships and appropriate interpretation and use of evaluation findings.

Discussion Questions

- Who are the key stakeholders?
- What is important to understand about this evaluation context?
- What else would be beneficial to know about the context?

Act 1: Focusing of the Evaluation

As part of the evaluation capacity building process, EvalCapacity met one-on-one with each community partner in the health, education, and social-emotional learning areas. They met with all program staff to discuss their programs, gain input for a logic model for the SKY initiative, and identify ways to measure program outcomes. All partners were excited about the capacity building process and were motivated to improve their rigor and routinize their data collection and evaluation work. None of the organizations had a formal evaluator on staff and the organizations used simple satisfaction surveys and attendance numbers for reporting. In addition, many of the tools and processes created for SKY could be used in their other programming efforts beyond SKY, which meant this process would support the capacity and outcomes-reporting for multiple community partner programs. All community partners were engaged and excited for the work ahead.

Ms. Keesha Turner and the evaluation team coordinated a SKY initiative event with the partners. One of the organizations served as the host. The leaders and one staff member from each organization attended. The day began with Ms. Turner reminding the organizations of the Foundation's vision and commitment to this work, followed by EvalCapacity sharing with the partners what they had learned across the organizations, from a community needs assessment, and how they might use this information to come to consensus on common outcome measures. Victoria, Kontrell, and Emily knew this was a critical meeting to build relationships and model for the partners how they would be sharing information and how it would be used for decision-making. They had intentionally included strengths and assets across the organizations, in addition to areas for concern. Victoria opened the presentation and handed it over to Kontrell who walked the partners through the analysis and findings. At the end of the presentation, they provided an opportunity for questions and input.

Partner 1: I just want to say thank you for the wealth of information that you shared today. For me, it validates why I do what I do, what I need to keep doing, and where I can change to better support the community. That's powerful. Knowledge is power. So often when we fill out surveys, sit in interviews, or pass out surveys in the community, we never see the results. Today we did. I'll be honest, when you first came to me, I wasn't sure about all of this, but now I know you are for real. Thank you.

Partner 2: Yes, I want to echo that thank you. To be honest, I was nervous about coming today. I assumed that this would not be that productive and you were just going to ask us to collect more data for you, which I'd do because our organization needs the funds, but I really didn't expect this meeting to be helpful to me and my organization. Could I have a copy of this to share with my staff at our next meeting?

Kontrell: You are so welcome. We would be happy to send out the presentation for you to share. If you would like us to be there when you share with staff to address any questions they have, we would also be happy to do so.

Dr. Mack: I appreciate my colleagues here, but I just want you to think about the neighborhood that you are in. We have been told for so long and in so many ways about all the problems here that I don't want to be a part of talking about areas for improvement. As we move forward, I think we need to focus on our success stories. At FutureNetwork, we only collect success stories, because those are the stories our kids need to be a part of and those outside of this neighborhood need to hear. I know we ask our kids how satisfied they are with our programming, and they always say they love it. To me, that is what matters.

Victoria: Thank you, Dr. Mack. We will continue to document the successes of what you are doing! It is so important to provide personal experiences and stories to evaluation work. But we think you all do such great work that we also want to document more specific outcomes. As Ms. Turner explained, we also see the SKY initiative as an opportunity for you as organizations, all working in the same community, to learn from each other to improve your services and better collaborate to support youth.

Partner 1: I am looking forward to that aspect of this project, because I know we have worked in silos for way too long even though we are all working in the same neighborhoods supporting youth. I know we will have a lot to learn from each of you.

Victoria proceeded to lead the partners through an interactive activity to come to consensus on outcomes and brainstorm potential data collection tools based on what they were already doing and/or desired to do. Emily noticed that Dr. Mack first left to use the bathroom, and then later took a long phone call. Her staff member continued to participate at her table, but she sensed that Dr. Mack was resistant to participating.

Discussion Questions

- How do you build trust when you are an outsider to the community?
- In the context of ECB, what is the responsibility or approach an evaluator should take when they meet resistance?
- How does a culturally responsive evaluator respond to the concerns that Dr. Mack raises? What are the systems of power, privilege, and oppression to be addressed in this context?
- How do you think Dr. Mack's reaction to the initiative will affect stakeholders in her organization?
- During this initial meeting, which stakeholders' voices were privileged? Whose voices were not heard? To what extent did the evaluators engage the interests of various stakeholders?
- Is the evaluation team demonstrating interpersonal competencies? Why or why not?

Act 2: Building Relationships

Victoria and Emily parked in a local church parking lot, as instructed to do so by Dr. Mack, and crossed the street to a building which used to be a warehouse. They noticed the colorful FutureNetwork sign and could hear a pickup basketball game in progress, which confirmed they were in the right place. Emily had met with Dr. Mack and explained the importance of having multiple stakeholders involved in the work, including youth, staff, parents/guardians, volunteers, and community members. Dr. Mack had staff meetings, Board meetings with community members, and lots of informal contact with youth and families, but no existing spaces for these stakeholders to collaborate. Although they were hoping many stakeholders could attend the meeting to work on developing a logic model, they were not sure what to expect, since Dr. Mack quickly agreed to this meeting just a few days ago. When they stepped in the main doors, they could see a large conference room to the left. They were a few minutes early, so they made themselves at home, as Dr. Mack instructed. They decided to sit in the middle of the long conference table, as they wanted to avoid sitting at the ends, which may give the impression that they were in charge rather than there to collaborate.

Shortly after, staff members began to join and exchanged pleasant introductions with the evaluation team. Dr. Mack was one of the last to enter the room. When she did, the small chatter ended, and all eyes went to the head of the table where she took her place. Dr. Mack explained although she invited a board member, volunteer, and a few parents, they all had conflicts. She and her staff were not comfortable with youth being in this first meeting. The meeting ran smoothly with those present, and they quickly went through the agenda that they had jointly developed with Dr. Mack. In the meeting, they were able to do introductions, discuss the rationale for the evaluation project and EvalCapacity's approach to working with organizations. They were able to address questions and alleviate staff concerns based on prior negative experiences with evaluation taking so much work with no benefit to them. They were also able to develop a draft logic model, specific to FutureNetwork, through an interactive activity, and identify a key focus area for their program evaluation. They decided to shift from student satisfaction to student outcomes in healthy behaviors (i.e., improved healthy eating and physical activity), education (i.e., reduced summer slide in literacy), and socio-emotional development (i.e., self-regulation, conflict resolution, communication skills).

Victoria and Emily reflected on the meeting as they drove back to their office.

Victoria: So, what was your impression of the meeting?

Emily: I felt like we got a lot accomplished for a first meeting. It was amazing that so many staff were able to attend the meeting and listened intently, but now that I think about it the staff were fairly quiet. Not to mention that no other stakeholders were present and they were concerned about involving youth in this process. I'd like to hear more on various stakeholders' perspectives. I'm a little concerned we have a draft logic model and focus for the evaluation when I don't know if we really heard all the perspectives.

Victoria: I noticed that too. Dr. Mack sure runs a tight ship. I wonder if she may have gotten input from the staff and the other stakeholders before our meeting. Let's hope that she did.

Emily: Maybe. I think next time I'd like to do some brief one-on-one meetings. Do you think Dr. Mack would be OK with that?

Victoria: We explained today that part of our process is getting input from various stakeholders, and she seemed to value that, so I hope so. Maybe once they have built trust with us, they will support involvement with the youth. She did come around since our last large meeting and was supportive of the outcome measures the SKY initiative agreed to collect. I also hope she can help us connect with youth and parents.

Emily: Me too.

Discussion Questions

- During this initial meeting, which stakeholders' voices were privileged? Whose voices were not heard? To what extent did the evaluators engage the interests of various stakeholders?
- What could the evaluation team have done differently to ensure more stakeholders were involved in the meeting? What might be next steps for the evaluation to involve more stakeholders?
- Is the evaluation team demonstrating professional competencies? Why or why not?

Act 3: Method and Strategy for the Evaluation

Over the past three months, the EvalCapacity team worked with six organizations in the SKY initiative – two each in the areas of healthy behaviors, education, and social-emotional development – to develop shared outcomes and measurement tools, in addition to supporting individual organizations with the development of logic models and additional data collection efforts regarding program implementation and outcomes. Given the shared goals, the evaluation team supported individual organizations in developing goals that were aligned with their logic model outcomes and based on historical data collection and conversations with the program and Foundation staff. The intent was to help the organizations set achievable, measurable goals to work toward, such that the program could improve its impact, expand its reach, and make programmatic adjustments based on data. Youths were out of school and programming was in full swing, and so was the implementation of their evaluation plans.

Kontrell and Emily, on behalf of EvalCapacity, visited FutureNetwork weekly to ensure data were being collected, entered, and analyzed on a routine basis. They were also supporting staff to look at program implementation regarding SKY's outcomes-focused work. They always checked in with Kia first. Kia worked at the front desk. She had grown up in the community and had been a volunteer at FutureNetwork for over a decade. All the youths knew her and always greeted her with a smile. Besides Dr. Mack, she had been at the organization the longest, so she also knew all of the staff who came to her for any problems they had from a broken copy machine to needing help mediating a conflict between two youths.

If there was anyone that could manage and process the youth intake surveys during the first week of programming, it was Kia. Kontrell and Emily were eager to work with her on reviewing her data entry, and then teaching her how to run the report. Once they had the report, they planned to meet with Dr. Mack and her advisory group that had been established with staff, volunteers, board members, parents/guardians, and youths. Emily recalled how much effort it took to get this group established, but now the group was working well together and Dr. Mack seemed to be warming up to working with the advisory group. At this point in the summer, the central outcome to monitor was the number of youths they were engaging, and the extent to which they were engaging youth that would most benefit from the services that FutureNetwork provided. Kia was excited to show Kontrell and Emily her Excel file where she had entered all 50 intake forms.

Kontrell: Thanks, Kia! I knew you would be a fast learner with this.
Kia: I know a puzzled look when I see one. What did I miss? What aren't you saying?
Kontrell: Well . . . [Kontrell looked back at his notes] . . . I see 50 cases here, but the goal FutureNetwork set was 100 youth everyday.
Kia: One hundred! (laughing) We haven't ever seen anything close to 100 kids up in here the first week of summer.
Emily: But it was Dr. Mack that suggested that goal. It's what she committed to with the other partners and the foundation. We wanted this goal to be realistic. I know you haven't had any way of tracking who was showing up, but we assumed Dr. Mack would know.
Kia: Well, the staff would love to be reaching more kids. They have even said to Dr. Mack that the groups would run better with more kids.
Kontrell: So why aren't there more kids then? We know from the community survey and interviews with parents that they want these opportunities for kids.
Kia: [looking back at her computer screen] I've said too much already. You're going to have to talk to Dr. Mack about all this. It isn't my place to say.
Emily: Thanks again Kia.

Kontrell helped Kia run the report on the 50 youths. With the report in hand, Emily and Kontrell set off to the conference room to meet with the advisory group. Right before the meeting, Dr. Mack told Kontrell she had an emergency and was not able to join the meeting, but that they should proceed to meet with the group. Kontrell expressed his understanding and arranged to touch base with Dr. Mack via phone in a couple of days. When Kontrell passed the information on to Emily, she recalled that Dr. Mack was unable to attend the meeting last week too. They wondered if Dr. Mack was avoiding them. Dr. Mack did not seem interested in looking through the report Kia had just completed. The advisory group members were all waiting in the room, so Kontrell and Emily put their thoughts on hold and joined them.

In the meeting they shared the report. They were disappointed with the number of youths that had enrolled, too, but explained that it was not too late to reach out in the community. Staff also noted that the youth didn't like completing the form, and a couple of them did initially refuse until staff explained it further. They also noticed that none of the youth reported any past or current issues with mental health, which was a concern because they were interested in targeting these youths. The rest of the meeting was filled with much energy and passion brainstorming ways of engaging and reaching out to the youth in the neighborhood. The advisory group was committed to program innovations to support youth.

Kontrell and Emily walked out of FutureNetwork with mixed feelings. Kontrell shared with Emily his struggles working on this project. He identified as African American, but was an outsider to this neighborhood and organization. They had still been able to help Dr. Mack establish the advisory group and develop relationships with them. And yet, he sensed Dr. Mack did not trust him and was hesitant to value input from the advisory group. Emily agreed. She wondered if Dr. Mack may perceive these expectations as being imposed on her and her organization. FutureNetwork had no systematic infrastructure for evaluation nor decentralized leadership when they started. Even though the EvalCapacity team and Foundation want to partner and collaborate with the organizations, from Dr. Mack's perspective, Emily recognized that they had a lot of power and influence over funding decisions, which may seem out of Dr. Mack's control. On the other hand, Kontrell reiterated that he thought FutureNetwork had capacity to reach more youth than they were currently. Was the intake survey culturally inappropriate? Could it be creating a barrier for youth starting the program? And what about their process of identifying shared outcomes and setting goals? Kontrell and Emily felt like they had developed open, trusting relationships with Kia and advisory group members, even though they were less sure about his relationship with Dr. Mack. They decided to reach out to Victoria about this prior to his phone call with Dr. Mack.

Discussion Questions

- How do race relations influence power and privilege in this evaluation context?
- To what extent and what ways are Kontrell and Emily being culturally responsive?
- What should the EvalCapacity team do next?
- Is the evaluation team demonstrating professional and interpersonal competencies? Why or why not?

Act 4: Evaluation Findings

At the end of the program, all data collection tools were implemented, collected, and analyzed. One month after the end of the program, EvalCapacity had a draft report of the findings for each organization. The data showed that attendance was highly variable at FutureNetwork. There were over 200 students who attended one day of the program; however, only ten students who attended 20+ days of a 30-day program. Interviews with program partners found that parents were not contacted when students were absent and that the change in students each day made it difficult to have consistency with groups and blunted the impact of layered lesson plans that built on each other.

Program outcomes were not strong. For healthy behaviors, there was a small, statistically insignificant increase in student knowledge about healthy eating habits and improved attitudes about eating healthy foods; however, there was negligible impact on actually eating more healthy foods at home. Similarly, students did not report improved physical activity outside of the summer program but did report a greater knowledge of physical activity and its relationship to healthier life outcomes. Social-emotional learning data showed similar outcomes – small changes in knowledge and attitude gain but no real changes in behavior. All increases were small, statistically insignificant, with negligible effect sizes.

Education data were also mixed. Students received literacy instruction for 90 minutes every day of the program – educational dosage was higher than either health or social-emotional learning dosage, both 60 minutes each. Therefore, the education program data were central to program efficacy. The education data were two-fold – teacher-implemented assessments of reading levels and, when school starts back up again, a comparison of students' standardized assessments from Spring to Fall to understand how the program mitigated "summer slide." The reading assessment showed that students generally stayed on the level they came into the program reading at, suggesting that the program helped mitigate summer slide; however, the standardized assessment data, which would more rigorously measure summer slide, would not be available until the Fall.

Outside of program impact, EvalCapacity also looked at program implementation. Through consistent meetings with program partners, observations of the program, and formal focus groups with various stakeholders, EvalCapacity identified multiple programmatic issues, many focused on program leadership, which persisted throughout the initiative despite efforts to share and address these concerns.

FutureNetwork had multiple assets, including but not limited to: a strong program coordinator, staff dedicated to and embedded within the community, and an innovative and promising program model.

At the same time, issues with FutureNetwork begin with leadership. FutureNetwork was a top-down, hierarchical organization led by Dr. Mack, whose leadership style focused on micro-management and small details; she was not open to any changes or suggestions for program model improvements; suggestions and program tweaks were quickly dismissed. New ideas and new ways of doing or thinking about the program were not encouraged; there was strong resistance to change, even if there were staff, community members, and youth consensus for change. For example, when a new logic model was developed for the program, many staff wanted to change programming to be more aligned to specific outcomes and felt the older logic model was out of date and not descriptive of the current work. Dr. Mack felt that "they already do these things" and shut down substantive conversation. This was a frequent refrain. Dr. Mack was resistant to change because she did not see the need for it; this stifled the ability of the program model to adapt and thrive. A clearly articulated organizational structure, with clearly defined roles and responsibilities, would also greatly benefit the program.

All of this led to an organizational culture that was top-down, lacked accountability, and did not encourage innovation, new ideas, or open dialogue. Dr. Mack's inability or unwillingness to recognize and/or address these issues made programmatic success difficult. The goal of FutureNetwork is to promote youth outcomes; however, current programming did not provide targeted dosage to drive toward these outcomes. Without resolution to these issues, FutureNetwork's work and impact would continue to be at a surface, rather than substantive, level.

Discussion Questions

- What is the best way to frame and communicate these findings, as a whole, for Dr. Mack, the advisory group, and Foundation? How should the evaluators address the implementation and leadership issues?

- In the context of an evaluation capacity building approach, what does an evaluator do when organizational leadership does not authentically value building and utilizing evaluation systems to engage in program improvement?
- How does the evaluation team proceed while aiming to maintain and repair relational trust?
- With the evidence pointing to the FutureNetwork not effectively utilizing resources to benefit youth, what is the responsibilities of the evaluators, particularly knowing that this has been a neighborhood that historically has limited access to resources?
- How does the evaluation team acknowledge and address the power imbalances between the Foundation, evaluation team, and program? Within the program stakeholders?
- How does the evaluation team ensure professional and interpersonal trust?

Act 5: Evaluation Reporting

Once the initial analysis was conducted and drafted, the findings were sent out to the EvalCapacity team and Victoria set up an internal meeting was set up to discuss the results and the best way to frame and communicate the reporting with each of the various stakeholders. The program findings showed limited impact, as well as implementation and leadership issues. Based on the anecdotal evidence of program impact provided by Dr. Mack when they made their funding decision, the Foundation would expect more robust results and would likely be very disappointed in the findings. Each member of EvalCapacity had a different perspective on how to proceed.

Victoria believed that the program results were tentative and provided highly sensitive information that could be politically explosive for FutureNetwork. Because there was low attendance and therefore lower program dosage, Victoria felt that that the program results were inconclusive. Without proper dosage, the evaluation team was unable to really make a strong statement about efficacy. In addition, the advisory board wanted to change their programming to be more aligned to program outcomes; however, this work was thwarted by leadership's micro-management and lack of clear lines of communication and accountability. Victoria recommended writing all of this up in a report and have one-on-one meetings with all the organizational stakeholders to discuss the initial results and chart a way forward. The report would include recommendations to improve implementation and dosage and would not recommend program termination.

Kontrell believed that the data should be written up objectively and that the role of the evaluator was to present the findings, both program impact and implementation. Framing the data brought in subjectivities that were not the responsibility of the evaluator. The report should be disseminated to all key stakeholders at the same time. The program was ineffective, so Kontrell believed a recommendation should be made to discontinue funding for the program. Even though he valued grassroots organizations in the community, he had no tolerance for ineffective programs when resources did not translate into tangible outcomes and believed there were better investments the foundation could make within the neighborhood that would be in better service toward youth. He appreciated the relationships he had built in the program and felt that the various stakeholders were ready for change and to confront Dr. Mack and challenges with organizational leadership.

Emily had also developed strong relationships with SKY program staff and advisory group members. She believed the results were a valid interpretation of program impact; however, she felt that the implementation issues blunted the impact of the program. Emily recommended writing up the report; however, she also recommended having individual conversations with each member of the advisory group, as well as the Foundation and Dr. Mack, to present the findings in a brief overview, which would provide specific recommendations for improving the program. The main issues with leadership and program bureaucracy would not be included, although program dosage would. Emily planned to only bring these issues of leadership and program bureaucracy to Dr. Mack and the Foundation. She was worried, however, that the Foundation may not be patient with the program improvement process and instead decide to pull funding.

Discussion Questions

- Which, if any of these three options, is the best way forward? Are there other ways to present these findings other than those outlines above?
- How does an evaluator navigate funding decisions based on limited engagement in evaluation capacity building efforts and the use of evaluation for formative purposes? How should the evaluator advocate for various stakeholders involved? How does the cultural context play a role in both the power dynamics and ultimate decision-making process of the evaluation team?
- How do you balance data-informed decision-making with a need to be responsive to communities? Can you justify ending a program if not reaching outcomes and no other services exist?
- Which of these approaches (or another) might align with competent (as defined by all five domains) evaluation practice?

Summary of Ethical Issues

A central tension in this case is the differences in attitudes by program leadership, who did not want to make implementation changes, and advisory group members, who wanted to ensure the program was implemented to achieve specific outcomes. This can be a common issue in evaluation capacity building projects when there are differing levels of buy-in and engagement with the ECB process. Often, programs are excited to create more systems for evaluation and have data that speak to their impact; however, the work required to create and implement these systems can be cumbersome. Programs are often happy to create logic models and define outcomes; however, when it comes to explicitly changing practice to facilitate the logic model outcomes, there can be pushback. What should ECB practitioners do in this situation? How should ECB practitioners engage with organizations that ultimately do not want to facilitate meaningful change and capacity building? Is it ever appropriate for an external funder to mandate capacity building? What is the evaluator's responsibility to address power, privilege, and oppression in this context?

The culturally responsive evaluator seeks to reflect the assets, needs, and values of a community. In the above example, the community is predominantly African American. Victoria, Emily, and the Board of the foundation, however, are Caucasian and outsiders to the community. Although Kontrell and Ms. Turner are African American, they are outsiders to the community. This creates a very specific and common power imbalance, exacerbated by issues of systemic racial inequities. Given this context, how is the role and decision-making of the evaluation coach affected? How does an outsider navigate these issues in a way that is culturally responsive? What are the key ethical and evaluative issues that need to be addressed?

Post Script

In this section, we provide reflections on what we would do, and a rationale based on the guidelines for ECB and AEA resources previously mentioned. The intent of this reflection is not to provide the "right" answer (in fact we will provide two responses) as these incidents do not have clear solutions; rather, it serves to model for the reader on how to relate these professional resources to particular contexts.

Leanne's Response

Although evaluators need to respond to challenges as they arise in an evaluation project, evaluators can also learn from their failures to guide their practice for future evaluations and contexts (Hutchinson, 2019). This practice supports "cultivating a life of the mind for practice," in which a practitioner "intentionally brings together theoretical understanding and practical reason, putting both to work in developing good judgment and taking a wise course of action" (Schwandt, 2020, p. 144). For this reflection, I want to focus on the ways in which the evaluation team was and was not culturally responsiveness in this setting, and what I might do differently with the next initiative. Before I start, I acknowledge that I most identify with Victoria, a White evaluation coach leading and mentoring other evaluators.

I want to acknowledge what I would continue doing again. I would continue to hire a diverse staff. Having Kontrell's input throughout the project was beneficial. Although he was not from this neighborhood, he provided critical support as the team worked in the neighborhood and developed relationships with the key stakeholders. Even still, we did not develop a trusting relationship with Dr. Mack, which is critical for being able to accept feedback and make changes. I could have actively and explicitly engaged in self-assessing and reflecting my own white privilege, modeling this for some of my staff. I could have done this with staff during our weekly check-ins. As an organization, I also need to hire or promote senior staff of color.

In all honesty, at EvalCapacity and the Foundation the efforts to seek participation from the organizations and build capacity was to foster use of the findings to promote program improvement. Fundamentally, we were doing what Cousins and Whitmore (1998) refers to as "practical participatory evaluation," which is rooted in practical problem solving. Such approaches do not fully recognize the dynamics of power in the context, which if I had been fully listening to Dr. Mack early on in the project, I would have been more attuned to addressing.

When the next program officer approaches me about ECB in an under-resourced neighborhood, I would have an educative conversation on the distinction between "practical participatory evaluation" and "transformative participatory evaluation." I would also explain that capacity building only works if an organization wants to do it. It does not work when mandated to do so with funding attached. If a foundation wants this type of accountability, which may be warranted, I would recommend having two separate evaluation firms – one leading ECB and one leading an external evaluation. The evaluation teams could still collaborate, but there would be minimal data sharing at the individual partner level from the ECB team to the external evaluation team. Partners need to know that they can generate evidence regarding their failures without being concerned about their funding being impacted.

I would also educate the Foundation and its Board on the need to address power imbalances, assuming that they truly wanted to build capacity in the community. A transformative approach would require a different role for a Foundation and a Board as they give more voice and ownership in the process than in the current arrangements. The Foundation, Board, and evaluators would need to listen and learn, and look for ways to advocate for systemic policy changes at the city and state levels that affect the communities. Outcomes for the youth programming would be exclusively defined by the community, rather than a negotiation between community and funder.

Also, we did the initial community needs assessment primarily working with Foundation staff to be efficient at the start of the project. Next time, I would encourage the Foundation to slow down the process and build in the community partners from the beginning. Although we sought community input when developing the logic models and identifying data collection tools for shared outcomes, we rooted this work in what we learned in the community needs assessment, which had not been developed in collaboration with community. Consequently, we were not consistently using culturally appropriate methods and language. A transformative participatory evaluation is rooted in traditions of critical theory, and such approaches have a rich tradition in utilizing stories as knowledge. Mertens and Wilson (2018) provided a comprehensive resource on data collection tools that have been utilized in transformative approaches to evaluation. For example, rather than using surveys and focus groups, we could have complemented surveys with a community poetry slam or photovoice project. I wonder if we had utilized alternative approaches to elicit stories, if the evaluation team and foundation staff might have understood the impact of FutureNetwork, which was outside of the unified outcomes that were identified for SKY. I wonder if Dr. Mack might have heard and been convicted to make some changes in her organization to hear the stories directly from youth in these settings.

Although we did not establish collaboration well at the start of the project, I would embed staff in the organizations again on a weekly basis throughout the project. In general, this approach fostered relationships and trust with stakeholders. More importantly, as outsiders of the neighborhood, we learned much about the culture in these organizations and communities.

Jay's Response

This is a complex evaluation situation; however, the issues outlined here are common experiences that evaluators face. Thoughtful deliberation on the ethical and professional implications of these issues is important for both novice and experienced evaluators. To arrive at my conclusions, I used ECB research, as well as the AEA Guiding Principles. My suggestions, of course, are not meant to be definitive – there are many ways to ethically and competently address these issues – but rather my personal lens at work, built on my own successes and challenges with these issues in the field. In addition, my response is through my personal lens as a White, male evaluator, who often leads projects in communities of color and is therefore in a powerful position. I want to recognize that my response may be influenced by my identity and power in unconscious ways.

Research on ECB has consistently shown that leadership buy-in to the process is critical for it to be successful (Labin et al., 2012; Silliman et al., 2016; Taylor-Powell & Boyd, 2008; Wade & Kallemeyn, 2020). Without leadership, ECB efforts can, and often do fail. Thus, developing a trusting relationship, built on shared values and a common purpose with Dr. Mack is critical to this project's success. She needs to see the evaluation efforts as a benefit for her vision, which takes a direct effort on the evaluation team to build a trusting rapport and relationship with her. AEA Competencies 5.1 and 5.4 encourages evaluators to build trusting relationships throughout the evaluation. Often, I try to build good will toward leadership by taking on extra responsibilities within the evaluation process – helping with other program logic models, showing up to community meetings, or volunteering my time at the organizations to show that I am "in it" with them, acting in good faith, and want the evaluation to advocate for the program/organization. These efforts build trust and can mitigate pushback on programmatic change suggestions and evaluation tools and outcomes.

In addition, ECB research shows that that using evaluation findings and seeing the benefits of that use can impact buy-in and change (Preskill & Boyle, 2008; Wade & Kallemeyn, 2020). Thus, while the initial results are disappointing, there are clear ways to improve the program in the future and, coupled with the leadership suggestions above, specific ways to alleviate issues of distrust. In this way, I would see these findings as an opportunity for growth and, with the adaptation of specific recommendations (i.e., improve attendance, align program activities to behavior change), a way to show staff and program partners that evaluation findings, when applied in future iterations of a program, can have tangible benefits to their work and be in service to their values, mission, and community. As such, I would present these results in an asset-based way, showing that there are clear ways to achieve the impact they want, and create enthusiasm for future growth of the program. At the onset of the effort, I would also couch evaluation as "a flashlight not a sledgehammer," to create a culture of data-as-learning rather than a culture fearful that data will be used as retribution. Similarly, I would try to work with SKY program to set goals and action plans to work towards improving some of these implementation issues, to ensure that goals and actions are implemented in service of improved impact.

Finally, while all AEA competencies apply in this scenario, E5. "Mitigate the bias and potential power imbalances that can occur as a result of the evaluation's context. Self-assess one's own privilege and positioning within that context" struck me as the most salient. This ECB and evaluation effort have lots of power imbalances – a foundation infusing large amount of money and expecting quick results with grassroots organizations, a neighborhood with a history of systemic racial and economic injustice, and evaluators with different racial backgrounds making key programmatic judgments about a community of Black children and families. All these imbalances deserve to be brought into conversation among stakeholders to guide the work. As evaluators, historical contexts are critically important to identify and address when presenting findings and working with organizations; and funders should strive to work collaboratively, in the interest of Common Good and Equity, with the grantees.

In addition, AEA competency 5.7 encourages culturally responsive interactions throughout an evaluation. Community members and parents were only involved in a surface level way – through a community assessment lightly mentioned in the text and a few representatives on the advisory group. If parents and other community members were actively involved in the ECB effort, their voices may have helped Dr. Mack be more open to change; they also may have brought up new ways of thinking about this work that went unmentioned in this example. Thus, it is important for ECB practitioners to frame the work as an ongoing, iterative process in service to community, and involved the community, such that a single year of programmatic outcomes does not strip away funding for a program. Being upfront about these issues with both the funder and the grantee can go a long way to set clear expectations for the program and show everyone that ECB work is in service to others.

Conclusion

Each evaluation project is rich in learning opportunities. We can learn from the experiences of others and our own. This case integrated reflection and discussion questions along the way, and it is also critical for evaluators to be engaging in ongoing reflection on their practice. This case also demonstrated ethical challenges that arise in a project that focuses on evaluation capacity building.

Note

1 This case is fictional, yet rooted in the experiences from multiple evaluation capacity building projects that each author independently led. We have based this case on documentation – evaluation plans, logic models, reports and other communications – for these projects. We have chosen to fictionalize the case to protect confidentiality of the stakeholders involved and ensure that we can articulate the ethical challenges that were encountered.

References

American Evaluation Association. (2011). *American Evaluation Association statement on cultural competence in evaluation*. Retrieved from www.eval.org/ccstatement

Compton, D. W., Baizerman, M., & Stockdill, S. D. (Eds.). (2002a). The art, craft, and science of evaluation capacity building. *New Directions for Evaluation, 93*.

Compton, D. W., Glover-Kudon, R., Smith, I. E., & Eden Avery, M. (2002b). Ongoing capacity building in the American Cancer society (ACS) 1995–2001. *New Directions for Evaluation, 2002*(93), 47–62.

Cousins, J. B., & Whitmore, E. (1998). Framing participatory evaluation. *New Directions for Evaluation, 1998*(80), 5–23.

Ensminger, D. C., Kallemeyn, L. M., Rempert, T., Wade, J., & Polanin, M. (2015). Case study of an evaluation coaching model: Exploring the role of the evaluator. *Evaluation and Program Planning, 49*, 124–136.

Hilton, L., & Libretto, S. (2017). Evaluation capacity building in the context of military psychological health: Utilizing Preskill and Boyle's multidisciplinary model. *American Journal of Evaluation, 38*(3), 393–404.

Hood, S., Hopson, R. K., & Frierson, H. (Eds.). (2014). *Continuing the journey to reposition culture and cultural context in evaluation theory and practice*. IAP.

Hood, S., Hopson, R. K., & Kirkhart, K. E. (2015). Culturally responsive evaluation. In K. E. Newcomer, H. P. Hatry, & J. S. Wholey (Eds.), *Handbook of practical program evaluation*. Wiley. https://doi.org/10.1002/9781119171386.ch12

Hutchinson, K. (2019). *Evaluation failures: 22 tales of mistakes made and lessons learned*. SAGE.

King, J. A. (2002). Building the evaluation capacity of a school district. *New Directions for Evaluation, 2002*(93), 63–80.

Labin, S. N., Duffy, J. L., Meyers, D. C., Wandersman, A., & Lesesne, C. A. (2012). A research synthesis of the evaluation capacity building literature. *American Journal of Evaluation, 33*(3), 307–338.

Mertens, D. M., & Wilson, A. T. (2018). *Program evaluation theory and practice*. Guilford Publications.

Neubauer, L. C., McBride, D., Guajardo, A. D., Casillas, W. D., & Hall, M. E. (2020). Examining issues facing communities of color today: The role of evaluation to incite change. In L. C. Neubauer, D. McBride, A. D. Guajardo, W. D. Casillas, & M. E. Hall (Eds.), *Examining issues facing communities of color today: The role of evaluation to incite change* (New Directions for Evaluation, vol. 166, pp. 7–11).

Nielsen, S. B., Lemire, S., & Skov, M. (2011). Measuring evaluation capacity – Results and implications of a Danish study. *American Journal of Evaluation, 32*, 324–344. https://doi.org/10.1177/1098214010396075

Preskill, H., & Boyle, S. (2008). A multidisciplinary model of evaluation capacity building. *American Journal of Evaluation, 29*(4), 443–459.

Schwandt, T. (2020). *Evaluation foundations revisited*. Stanford University Press.

Silliman, B., Crinion, P., & Archibald, T. (2016). Evaluation champions: What they need and where they fit in organizational learning. *Journal of Human Sciences and Extension, 4*(3).

Tarsilla, M. (2014). Evaluation capacity development in Africa: Current landscape of international partners' initiatives, lessons learned and the way forward. *African Evaluation Journal*, *2*(1), 13.

Taut, S. (2007). Studying self-evaluation capacity building in a large international development organization. *American Journal of Evaluation*, *28*(1), 45–59.

Taylor-Powell, E., & Boyd, H. H. (2008). Evaluation capacity building in complex organizations. In M. T. Braverman, M. Engle, M. E. Arnold, & R. A. Rennekamp (Vol. Eds.), *Program evaluation in a complex organizational system: Lessons from cooperative extension* (*New Directions for Evaluation, vol. 120*, pp. 55–69).

Valéry, R., & Shakir, S. (2005). Evaluation capacity building and humanitarian organization. *Journal of Multi-disciplinary Evaluation*, *2*(3), 78–112.

Wade, J., & Kallemeyn, L. (2020). Evaluation capacity building (ECB) interventions and the development of sustainable evaluation practice: An exploratory study. *Evaluation and Program Planning*, *79*, 101777.

Wade, J., Kallemeyn, L., Ensminger, D., Baltman, M., & Rempert, T. (2016). The Unified Outcomes Project: Evaluation capacity building, communities of practice, and evaluation coaching. *The Foundation Review*, *8*(1), 5.

4 'Dream big, believe in yourself, and keep moving forward' ManaiaSAFE Forestry School Pilot Kaupapa Māori Evaluation

Marg Wilkie, Christine Roseveare and Henry Koia

Introduction

From te ao Māori (the Māori world), and like a bird sitting on one's shoulder, a manaia is a stylised figure representing a guardian that crosses between the spiritual and human worlds (Te Aka Māori Dictionary). A manaia appears in the logo of the ManaiaSAFE Forestry School (MFS) that created a new safety-based training course for the forestry industry of Aotearoa New Zealand, the most lethal workplace in the country (WorkSafe, 2020). A Kaupapa Māori evaluation gathered evidence from the 20-week MFS pilot course in 2018–2019 that trained 11 tauira (trainees).

An insight into important elements of a successful evaluation in this particular setting can be seen in the following early 19th-century whakataukī (proverb) by wāhine rangatira (female chief) Meri Ngaroto (Te Aupouri) 'He aha te mea nui o te ao? He tāngata, he tāngata, he tāngata.' (What is the most important thing in the world? It is people, it is people, it is people). Readers are included in the important people, who will see this theme repeated in various ways throughout this case.

One aim of the evaluation was to inform decisions made by central government and other enabling stakeholders about ongoing funding and support for the development of the training programme. The methods and main learnings of the evaluation gave insight into the programme, the forestry industry, forestry training and safety, and the views of tauira, their whānau (families) and their Kaiako (teachers) and Kaiārahi (mentors).

Kaupapa Māori research practices and approaches developed in Aotearoa New Zealand were used for the MFS evaluation. The questions and methods used in the four phases of the evaluation were combined in a final report and for a presentation of the findings and learnings from the MFS pilot at their graduation.

In July 2018, a small Aotearoa New Zealand company trading as the MFS, based in Te Tairāwhiti (the shore where the light shines across the water) Gisborne, invited proposals for Kaupapa Māori research to evaluate their innovative pilot training programme.

Part of a Kaupapa Māori approach or viewpoint is in the smallest details, for example to order words in te reo Māori (language) followed by the English translations in brackets. This reflects the fact of Māori as tangata whenua (people of the land) using te reo Māori before the English language of the colonisers who arrived later. This case study starts with a whakataukī, a saying, that shares a core value of te ao Māori, a shared mātauranga (knowledge). Formal speeches in te ao Māori will often start with a whakataukī. Here chosen to include all readers worldwide and to signal the focus of the MFS evaluation. A useful resource for people wanting to understand more of Māori culture and language is the government funded Te Aka Māori Dictionary online (no date) which gives the multiple definitions of words i te reo (in the language) and a helpful audio link giving the sound of each word.

DOI: 10.4324/9780429277788-4

Māori cultural values were part of the Kaupapa Māori evaluation including; whanaungatanga (relationships), manaakitanga (care for each other), tikanga (correct ways), wairuatanga (spirituality), pūkengatanga (advisers) and kotahitanga (working collectively). These values as research and evaluation practice are discussed in more detail later. The Aotearoa New Zealand Evaluation Association (2019) values four similar guiding principles in evaluation standards including; establishing respectful meaningful relationships, ethic of care, responsive methodologies and trustworthy results. The MFS pilot evaluation navigated the values and principles from both approaches.

Background and Contexts

The MFS training was designed to address nationwide issues of forestry workforce supply, health and safety, and work-ready competencies for local and national forestry.

Research into forestry training by WorkSafe, Aotearoa New Zealand's primary workplace health and safety regulator, found nationwide the availability and quality was poor and was not meeting the needs of forest owners, contractors or crews. A lack of quality on-site trainers was linked to the low funding for trainers, seen as 'too low to attract trainers who had the experience and expertise needed' (WorkSafe New Zealand, 2017; Sinclair, 2017).

In February 2019, Prime Minister Jacinda Ardern spoke of plans to change vocational training with far reaching changes to the Institutes of Technology and Polytechnics (ITPs). Sector wide structural issues of poor co-ordination and integration, a duplication of services and a lack of scale and capital needed to be addressed. 'We need to move away from the cycle that sees course delivery at institutes boom when the economic cycle turns down and then dive when the economy improves, while on-the-job training providers face the opposite cycle' (Radio NZ, 2019b).

On 14 February 2019 Minister of Education Hon. Chris Hipkins announced a final round of consultation on government proposals that would directly impact the forestry industry and forestry training. The Review of Vocational Education and Training (ROVE) included; the ITPs, the Industry Training Organisations (ITOs) and other Tertiary Education Organisations (TEOs) including Private Training Establishments (PTEs) and Wānanga (Māori universities). One idea was for the tertiary institutions to take over the job of organising and providing work-based industry training to 'promote better alignment between on- and off-job education and training, and stabilise provision of vocational education across the economic cycle' (Radio NZ, 2019a; Tertiary Education Commission, 2017).

The goal of the MFS pilot project evaluation was to provide evidence on the benefits or otherwise of this approach to training for forestry locally and nationwide. The findings in the report would help inform decisions on what, if anything, would eventuate beyond the pilot, including (1) whether Government and industry decision makers would have the confidence to partner with MFS for scale-up; (2) whether the Government would instigate high-level evidence-based policy change that better delivers skills for the forest industry and (3) whether improvements to productivity and safety can be achieved in other industries such as horticulture through applied learning (Wilkie, 2018).

An innovative feature of the MFS training model was access to a unique forest-based training environment that supports a Māori Kaupapa (philosophy) practice and delivery model. For this reason, Kaupapa Māori research was preferred for the evaluation as it could best fit and recognise the cultural values and practices of the training programme.

In the forest, new entrants to the forestry industry were mentored by highly experienced bushmen under strict supervision, often 1:1. The MFS training was designed to ensure (no date) the new entrants had the knowledge, skills, experience and values to stay safe, before walking onto a commercial logging site (Koia, 2018a, p. 7). An innovative aspect of the training model was the pilot could create income from the high-quality logs harvested by the trainees and their mentors.

The MFS pilot project was essentially about testing the feasibility of the training model. The project put 11 new-entrant trainees through a 20-week cable harvesting training programme. The graduates would hold the New Zealand Certificate in Forest Harvesting Operations (Level 3) with strands in tree-felling and quality control, breaking-out cable, or manual processing and quality control (Koia, 2018a, p. 7). All of the trainees in the initial training programme were Māori.

Funding for the MFS pilot was provided by 'enabling stakeholders', project investors Te Uru Rākau – Forestry New Zealand using the Provincial Growth Fund; Eastland Community Trust (now Trust Tairāwhiti) and the Forest Growers Levy Trust. Tertiary Education Commission (TEC) funding was accessed by Te Aho a Māui – Eastern Institute of Technology (EIT) that partnered with MFS to run the pilot. A contract with EIT enabled the Level 3 Forestry qualifications to be gained 'off the job' (Wilkie, 2018).

The July 2018 Request for Proposals for the evaluation was three months ahead of the 'not yet quite fully funded' MFS pilot starting in October. The evaluation was one small part of the strategic plan of the MFS project. The MFS pilot evaluation was expected to provide the critical knowledge needed 'to give Government and industry decision makers the confidence to partner for scale-up and to initiate high-level evidence-based Government policy change to existing education and training aiming to better deliver skills for industry' (Wilkie, 2018, p. 18).

In August 2018 MFS contracted Dr Marg Wilkie, (Ngāti Porou, Ngāpuhi) for the evaluation. The Māori names in parentheses show Māori iwi (tribes) by whakapapa (descent). 'Dr Marg' was specifically selected for her Kaupapa Māori research and evaluation, vocational training and Māori education expertise, which provided the 'warrants' to make evaluative conclusions in this context (Nunns et al., 2015).

The timeframe for the evaluation was from 27 August 2018 to 29 March 2019. In the context of high expectations, and short timeframes one challenge was designing a robust evaluation process that was participative, respectful, empowering and would uphold cultural and evaluation practices. Central to this was adopting a Kaupapa Māori approach.

MFS Project Manager Henry Koia (Ruawaipu), and MFS Managing Director Steve Beach (Ruawaipu, Uepohatu) worked with Dr Marg to scope and design a Kaupapa Māori evaluation, to fit the available budgets of funds and time.

Kaupapa Māori

The MFS programme was a Kaupapa Māori intervention in education, vocational training and saving lives in the forest. At one level, Kaupapa Māori is simply 'about Māori' (Cram, 2016, 2018). Kaupapa Māori research is often described as 'by Māori, with Māori, for Māori' (Irwin, 1994), and in this case, at one level, it was. Kaupapa Māori also has significance nationally for all of Aotearoa New Zealand as a transformative practice, particularly in education (Smith, 1997).

Evaluation is one type of research undertaken under broader Kaupapa Māori research practice (Smith, 2012; Cram et al., 2015). It is often the case that Māori identify the most effective tools and methods to gather evidence to be used for specific purposes (Cram et al., 2018). For the MFS evaluation, the evidence gathered was to inform key stakeholders, including MFS itself, the trainees, their whānau and the MFS enabling funders and sponsors.

As explained in the Rangahau (Research) online resource, Kaupapa Māori refers to an approach, framework or methodology for thinking about and undertaking research.

It is about having a kaupapa (topic or issue) to research. Kaupapa Māori research often addresses issues of injustice and of social change (Rangahau, n.d.).

'Kaupapa Māori research takes into account historical Māori experiences with research' previously often done to and about us, not often with, by and for us. 'Kaupapa Māori research focuses on Māori culture, language, values, history, people and contemporary realities' (Rangahau, n.d.). Kaupapa Māori guided the methods used in the MFS evaluation.

Overview of the Evaluation Approach

The MFS evaluation was designed in four phases:

1   Scoping and Initial Review
2   Kaupapa Māori Social Cost Benefit Analysis
3   ManaiaSAFE Forestry School Pilot Formative Evaluation
4   ManaiaSAFE Forestry School Pilot Evaluation Final report

Table 4.1 summarises the overall evaluation questions asked in each phase, and the methods used to answer them.

Phase 1: Scoping and Initial Review

A review of literature of national and regional forestry training defined the need for high-quality training. The scope identified the large number of forest-related government agencies, and the lack of shared cohesive policy. Review of MFS strategic plans and documentation identified the foundational values and Māori Kaupapa approach to the pilot. MFS co-designed the Kaupapa Māori evaluation clearly aimed at informing government decision makers and the enabling stakeholders supporting the MFS pilot.

Phase 2: The Kaupapa Māori Cost-Benefit Analysis

The MFS evaluation included a Cost-Benefit Analysis (CBA), as the second phase of the evaluation. This aimed to contribute evidence of the value of the MFS programme for consideration by government agencies financially supporting the development of the programme. The first step of a CBA is to identify the problem and establish the 'do nothing counterfactual' (Treasury, 2015). The counterfactual defines a baseline of 'if the government did nothing and if there is no intervention'. This step is a prerequisite in government financial and policy making decisions.

The Kaupapa Māori CBA placed the MFS pilot in a national context, using the 'do nothing counterfactual' used by decision makers to commit government funding to new initiatives. The Treasury (2018a, 2018b, 2018c) tool 'CBAx', is loaded with values used to monetise the potential impact the MFS training as an intervention. For example, in 2019 values, the social cost of being unemployed was calculated for each person at NZ$69,186 a year. When 8 MFS rookies graduated in to work, there was a yearly total benefit of NZ$414,696, about half the cost of the pilot training programme.

A distinctive feature of the Kaupapa Māori CBA analysis was challenging a 'deficit thinking' used in the past to describe and explain the differences between Māori and others. For example, a deficit view of the programme context might focus on deprivation.

Table 4.1 MFS Pilot Evaluation Summary of Questions and Methods

Phase	Overall evaluation questions	Methods
1 Scoping and Initial Review	What is the kaupapa of the MFS programme? What is the wider context? Why is this programme needed?	Review of MFS strategic plans and documentation Review of literature of national and regional forestry training and forest related government agencies Co-designed evaluation in consultation with MFS.
2 Kaupapa Māori Social Cost Benefit Analysis	What potential value does the MFS training add in monetary terms? How worthwhile is it in terms of the resources put in (value for money)?	Analysis using the Treasury (2018a, 2018b) tool 'CBAx' that monetised the value of the MFS training.
3 MFS Pilot Formative Evaluation	How well designed and implemented is this programme?	Review of project documentation and interviews with 'enabling stakeholders' including the Eastern Institute of Technology and Earnslaw One. Mapping the foundation of MFS including the central government funding and the other local businesses and agencies that supported the development of the programme.
	How valuable are the outcomes of the MFS programme and this learning experience to trainees, their whānau and their communities? How well does it provide opportunities and address their needs and aspirations?	Co-creating filmed interviews with tauira (trainees) to capture the voices of their fellow trainees, their whānau (families), their Kaiako (teachers) and their forest-based mentors. Transcripts were thematically analysed. The evaluation design generated baseline information and tools for use in self-review and self-evaluation in ongoing MFS training.
4 MFS Pilot Evaluation final report	How well does MFS address the problems identified in the wider context?	The MFS final report summarises all of the evaluation findings and learnings, judging the existing value of the programme, according to its main participants and stakeholders, including the baseline findings of the CBA and Formative Evaluation. The results and learnings were shared with all participants and stakeholders, as reports, an audio-visual presentation to the graduation, and images and film records returned to MFS.

On a scale of 1–10 of the New Zealand Index of Deprivation, most of Te Tairāwhiti region, where ManaiaSAFE was based, is at 10, the most deprived (Atkinson et al., 2014).

Census data report the estimated resident population in Gisborne, at 30 June 2017 as 48,500. In 2013, Māori were 48.9% of the Gisborne regional population, the highest regional proportion of people identifying as Māori in Aotearoa New Zealand. In September 2018, 5,240 people in Gisborne were receiving central government support from benefits. Māori were over-represented at 4,031 or 70% of those receiving benefits. One of the lowest GDP per capita across all of Aotearoa is found in the Gisborne region at the minimum rate of NZ$39,896 per annum (Wilkie, 2019a).

The NEET rate is the total number of youths (aged 15 to 24 years) who are not in education, employment, or training, as a percentage of the total youths working-age population. The Ministry of Business, Innovation and Employment reported the national NEET rates to June 2018 as 11.6%. In Gisborne the NEET rate was 21.8%, almost twice the national rate. This pattern of difference is repeated in other areas of high Māori population.

One of the considerations for the Kaupapa Māori evaluation was to provide information supporting the potentials or otherwise of the MFS training model to transform these realities (Koia, 2018b).

As a high-risk industry where deaths occur too often (Radio New Zealand, 2020a, 2020b), the costs of the loss of a life have been monetised in the CBAx. The Statistical Value of Life, an amount calculating the average cost of one life lost was NZ$4.71 million for 2018. WorkSafe NZ (2020) reports in 2018, there were six deaths in Forestry and Logging, and in 2019 another seven fatalities. The MFS pilot was impacted by three of the deaths during the evaluation. The CBA put the costs of the MFS intervention into a perspective when lives are potentially saved through safety and other skills training (Wilkie, 2019a).

While the evaluation used the concept of the counterfactual and the preloaded monetary values of the CBAx framework to frame expenditure on MFS as an intervention, it also suggested models that could be used in future to value benefits of Kaupapa Māori-based programmes, as 'CBA is unable to effectively integrate qualitative and indigenous values' (Treasury, 2015). Acknowledging the time limits on the evaluation, two recommended frameworks for future evaluation work included the work of Tā (Sir) Mason Durie (Rangitāne, Ngāti Kauwhata, Ngāti Raukawa) called Te Whare Tapa Wha (the four-sided house) (1994). This model is used in many Aotearoa New Zealand sectors, including education, and known to government decision makers. It considers four linked attributes of holistic well-being for Māori and others; te taha hinengaro (mental well-being); te taha whanau (family and social well-being); te taha wairua (spiritual well-being) and te taha tinana (physical well-being). These values were demonstrated in practice in the MFS pilot programme (Koia, 2018a, Status Report 2, p17).

The other framework suggested was the indigenous Mauri model developed by Engineer Dr Te Kipa Kepa Morgan (Ngati Pikiao of Te Arawa) that measures the mauri or life force in four dimensions; taiao mauri (environmental wellbeing); hapu mauri (cultural well-being) hapori mauri (social well-being) and whānau mauri (economic well-being). The Mauri model 'provides a method for supporters and funders of projects to take account of cultural considerations. The idea is that mauri, rather than money measures how sustainable a project is. Using mauri is more accurate and useful than merely counting the cost' (Morgan, 2006).

Phase 3: The Formative Evaluation

The Formative Evaluation, Phase 3 of the research for the MFS pilot, documents the contexts and development of the MFS primarily through review of literature, project documentation and interviews.

An important contractual requirement of the MFS pilot evaluation was to ensure the voices of the participants and their families were heard. This phase of the evaluation pays particular attention to this aspect and so we spend some time on it. The Kaupapa Māori approach engaged the trainees and MFS trainers and mentors as participants and co-creators of their own evaluations and also engaged with whānau and other key participants and contributors. It was collaboratively designed to generate a baseline of information and a series of tools that could be used in self-evaluation of ongoing MFS training.

During week 4 of the MFS pilot, Dr Marg facilitated a wānanga training and learning day with the rookie loggers and some of their Kaiako (teachers). Training was held at the MFS pilot site of the Eastern Institute of Technology Tairāwhiti Rural Studies Campus, in Stout Street, Gisborne. This timing was for Dr Marg to engage the trainees before they went into the forest. Pre-dawn on the same day Tohunga (priests, experts) of Te Aitanga-a-Mahaki and others, gathered with Kaiako and Kaiārahi (mentors) of the MFS pilot, preparing the way to safety for the forest-based real-world training. MFS gave permission to write about these sacred matters here, and one mentioned 'the birdsong was the loudest I have ever heard'.

A presentation based around a computer-generated movie about how Māori tertiary students achieve their academic and qualification goals was recognised by many of the trainee rookies as reflecting in parts their own stories. Discussions about what research is and why the MFS pilot is being evaluated, led on to a process to achieve fully informed consent and release for publications of their words, thoughts, images and movies in the evaluation and for other presentation, promotional or educational purposes. Project Manager for the MFS evaluation, and co-author Henry Koia, gave specific permission on behalf of MFS for use of the evaluation reports in this case study, and access to the MFS progress status reports to funders.

As part of the Kaupapa Māori evaluation transformative approach, with shared understanding of the critical purposes of the evaluation, the MFS pilot rookies were actively involved co-creating questions to ask of each other, their teachers and mentors and their whānau. During the day, filmed interviews were trialled by the trainees, and after viewing and critiquing all the films as a group, the interviews were redone to capture a better understanding of their current learning experiences inside the MFS pilot. Transcripts of their words appear as qualitative evidence of the value of the MFS training to them, their whānau and their communities. A thematic analysis was used to order the information.

A rapid-fire self-evaluation asked everyone to reflect on their experiences for the day and to give a single word to describe it. Arranged alphabetically, their words are: Awesome; Cool; Creative; Exciting; Learning; Massive; 'Meke (Tumeke surprised); Participation; Proud; PUMPING!' These words as self-evaluation and review can also describe the MFS training programme pilot, the tauira (trainees) and their Kaiako in Week 4 (Wilkie in Koia, 2018b).

A second round of filmed interviews completed by the Log 9 Rookies with their fellow trainees, their whānau and their forest-based mentors took place in weeks 19 and 20 of the pilot. Dr Marg also interviewed key contributors to the pilot who represent some of the major stakeholders. The interviews were transcribed and edited, analysed and coded thematically to create and disseminate the evaluation results and learnings to all participants and stakeholders, as reports, an audio-visual presentation to the graduation, and image and film records.

Phase 4: The MFS Pilot Final Report

The MFS pilot evaluation final report includes summaries of all the evaluation findings and learnings that present evidence judging the existing value of the programme, according to its main participants and stakeholders, alongside the baseline findings of the CBA (Wilkie, 2019a) and Formative Evaluation (Wilkie, 2019b).

Some Reflections on Kaupapa Māori Evaluation in Practice

Whanaungatanga (Relationships)

Māori have a way of viewing tangata whenua (people of the land) as part of an interconnected web of whanaungatanga (relationships), which extend beyond people to the natural environments. Both the MFS pilot programme and evaluation project used processes of whakawhanaungatanga (establishing relationships) that continued long after the training and evaluation was completed. In a Māori way, relationships can be established for example through existing kin relationships at a whānau, local community or iwi (tribal) level. Understanding and being part of this network of relationships in te Ao Māori with insider status is of great value, and may even be necessary, for an evaluator to work effectively in a Maori context, but it also means conflicts of interest may need to be considered.

As a member of Ngāti Porou, the largest iwi in Te Tairāwhiti, Dr Marg had assumed there would be a strong likelihood of a kinship relationship with one or more of the key participants of the programme. This potential conflict of interest saw Ratahi Cross, the Chairman of the MFS Board, a cousin kin of Dr Marg, stand down while all decisions about the evaluation research contract were made. The earlier death of a mutual cousin, Robin Chaffey, in the forest, was also declared as potential bias of kinship and subjectivity.

In some evaluation approaches, an objective or outsider status for the evaluators may be preferred. For kairangahau Māori (researchers) doing evaluations, when working with Māori, by virtue of being Māori, the objective status is not often obtainable (Cram, 2016). However, the MFS Board of Directors did not see this as an issue, as they engaged an independent, qualified, and experienced Kaupapa Māori researcher and evaluator from outside of the community and the region. The shared understanding of Kaupapa (philosophy), whakapapa (geneology) and kawa (protocols) were shared foundations for the evaluation to proceed.

Manaakitanga (Hospitality and Care of Others)

Both the MFS training programme and the evaluation practically applied the core Māori value of manaakitanga (the respect and care of others). The manaakitanga included extra direct care and pastoral support of the individual trainees, that extended out to the relationships of care between the forestry mentors employed by MFS and the Log 9 Rookies of the 2018–2019 pilot.

Unexpectedly, manaakitanga became more critical during the final 3 months of the evaluation, due to an eyesight impairment. Dr Marg decided to declare this issue and offer to stand down from the evaluation. In discussion with the MFS Board that offer was declined and the care issues resolved by MFS Director Christine Beach (Ruawaipu), volunteering as driver and transport for Dr Marg to complete the final round of stakeholder, whānau and participant interviews.

The MFS manaakitanga extended to the set-up of a whānau barbecue and fun day at the Gisborne Olympic Pool Complex where the tauira filmed their own interviews with mentors and whānau. MFS also set up the final pilot evaluation event reporting the findings and celebrating the achievements of the programme and the newly qualified foresters graduating the pilot. Guest speakers included te reo speaker Gisborne Mayor Meng Foon, who was appointed New Zealand Race Relations Commissioner in 2019.

Tikanga (Right Ways)

Tikanga can be explained as the correct ways to approach and do things. The word tika means right or correct. However, tikanga is subtly different in specific places, within local communities and between iwi. The Kaupapa Māori approach of the evaluation was deliberately chosen as it resonated with the tikanga in Te Tairāwhiti, and the tikanga of the MFS pilot. For example, there are correct tikanga to approach the plantation forests and trees that are about to be harvested.

Wairuatanga (Spirituality)

In common with other indigenous peoples, for many Māori, spirituality is an essential part of life and may be embedded within indigenous programmes and services. Culturally, responsive evaluation in a Māori context includes enquiring about, acknowledging and reporting on the spiritual aspects of the programme (Kennedy et al., 2015).

The forest-based training location of the MFS Pilot was in the Mangatu forest, within Te Aitanga-a-Mahaki (descendants of Mahaki) tribal rohe (area). Tohunga (wise and experienced experts) belonging to tangata whenua (here the local people of the land) Te Aitanga-a-Mahaki and others, came in from locations inside and outside the region, to bless the site, seeking spiritual supports and freedom from injury and deaths that are a constant concern in forestry. Only males were present on the MFS training site pre-dawn and at the falling of the first tree that was part of the blessing. This event was not reported in the evaluation, but understood as a prerequisite for the commencement of the forest-based training. The MFS evaluation suggests 21 themes for future research, including one to gather the stories of the spiritual elements of Forestry for Māori and tangata whenua, and all other foresters.

Pūkenga (Advisors)

Seeking the advice of knowledgeable kaumatua (elders) in an area where research or evaluation with tangata whenua is occurring is a helpful support for evaluators coming in from outside the area (Cram et al., 2018). Dr Marg had the help of Pae Arahi (Guides) who were acknowledged kaumatua (elders) for three sites of doctoral research (Wilkie, 2010). Drawing on a connection, made working for Te Whare Wānanga o Awanuiārangi, the indigenous university located in Whakatāne from 2011 to 2013, Dr Marg contacted Te Tairāwhiti resident respected kaumatua, Elder Te Reo (Ngāti Porou) for advice about the MFS pilot evaluation.

Discussions covered the current political, social and economic contexts in Te Tairāwhiti, some of the issues of concern for local iwi about health and education and about forestry regionally in particular. In June 2018, a 'one in 100 year' storm flooded the 'most erosion prone region in Aotearoa New Zealand', sending slash, one unsaleable by-product of forestry, sliding down hillsides and through waterways, destroying one house, damaging roads and cluttering rivers and beaches with rotting wood. On the beach in front of his home, Elder and his son had gathered and staked the largest slash log offcuts into a retaining wall, that soon after saved 20–30 meters of beachfront from eroding away in another storm.

Elder spoke of the impacts of forestry deaths on whānau, and the impacts of the exotic forest plantations on Papatūānuku (Earth Mother). Asked about what damage plantation forestry did to the environment, Elder explained whatever was planted and grew above the ground did not matter, if it nourished Papatūānuku and her whānau. On reflection, the forests are a product of Papatūānuku that in return supports and nourishes the local people (personal communication, Elder Te Reo, 19 November 2018).

Kotahitanga (Unity and Working Collectively)

Expressed on many levels within the MFS pilot, the evaluation captures and describes kotahitanga, or working collectively, in action. This begins with a shared vision, developed over a period of five years prior to the pilot starting. All of the pilot participants, the directors, trainers, and mentors, the 'enabling stakeholders' including funders and sponsors, local whānau and businesses and the self-titled 'Log 9 Rookies' themselves contributed to the collective work and success of the pilot.

Acknowledging the Real-World Contexts

At the time of the first MFS pilot assessments for numeracy and literacy levels, the death of a Māori 29-year-old pregnant local, in an accident with a logging truck, had impacted the MFS whānau, trainees and local communities. The preparation for tangi (funeral) clashed with and impacted on training and assessment sessions.

At the time of second literacy and numeracy assessments, the death of a logger in the forest outside of Tolaga Bay had severely personally impacted the MFS whānau, several of the rookies, MFS Board members, the local communities and the local logging industry. Other whānau events, known to the MFS mentors and teachers, were impacting individual rookies at the time of the research and the assessments. The context of forestry as one of the most lethal workplaces in Aotearoa New Zealand (WorkSafe, 2020) was a constant motivation for MFS to make a difference in their local forests, and potentially nationwide.

A Kaupapa Māori evaluation using a qualitative approach captured these impacts on the people in their bi-cultural real-world contexts as part of the evaluation report.

Overall Evaluation Findings

One overall goal of the MFS pilot project evaluation was to provide evidence on the benefits or otherwise of this approach to training for forestry locally and nationwide. The evaluation report would help inform decisions on what, if anything, would eventuate beyond the pilot, including (1) whether Government and industry decision makers would have the confidence to partner with MFS for scale-up; (2) whether the Government would instigate high-level evidence-based policy change that better delivers skills for the forest industry and (3) whether improvements to productivity and safety can be achieved in other industries such as horticulture through applied learning (Wilkie, 2018). The pilot evaluation was always part of the MFS Strategic Plan.

Key learnings from the evaluation included that 'every New Zealander is a stakeholder in our forests. Responsibility for government policy in forestry is spread over a number of government departments with no all-embracing forestry policy'. The scoping review identified '17 Crown Ministers, 38 Labour government portfolios, 23 separate Ministries and Crown Entities or Agencies as stakeholders in Forestry and 18 key targeted stakeholders of the MFS Pilot' (Wilkie, 2018).

Some insights from interviews with the tauira (trainees) who called themselves 'Log 9 Rookies' include the range of iwi represented on the programme, their reasons for enrolling, how they found out about it, what their whānau thought about it, the positives and negatives of the training, and their aspirations.

The main finding of the evaluation was that overall the MFS pilot evaluation 'strongly supports the claim that a National Network of MFS is likely to deliver significant socio-economic benefits to the forest industry and its supplier network, forest-based communities across the regions, Māori and Pasifika, and the national economy' (Wilkie 2019c).

The basis for the findings were, the level of support for the programme by MFS itself, the trainees and teachers, the mentors and stakeholders; the strength and quality of the MFS pilot design; its cultural validity; consideration of the do-nothing counterfactuals; the perceived value of the mentoring in the forest-based training; the partnership approach with enabling stakeholders and funders; and likely qualification and employment outcomes for participants compared to other training models. As all the Log 9 Rookies gained safety certificates, including fire safety and chainsaw safety as prerequisites to entering the forest there were clear benefits and potentials for improving health and safety in the forestry industry nationally and locally.

> The evaluation showed a total support for the MFS training in development and delivery, impacting significantly socio economically to the individual MFS Log 9 Rookie Loggers, their whānau, the MFS mentors and teachers, the MFS Directors and Board, the local Gisborne Forestry industry, and to the broader Te Tairāwhiti region. The findings of this small-scale research are not generalisable, the learnings from it are. The potentials for scale-up of the MFS project, to a nationwide network of MFS training are bright.
> (Wilkie, 2019c, p. 6)

And then What Happened?

On 2 April 2019, the front page of the regional newspaper The Gisborne Herald declared 'forestry pilot hailed a success' citing the findings of the MFS evaluation report.

The MFS motto is 'Dream big, believe in yourself, and keep moving forward', a collectively agreed direction for all participants and the wider MFS whānau. The MFS pilot demonstrated the changes needed in training for the forestry sector, starting with the most complex, challenging, and at times lethal, conditions in remote and inhospitable environments where trees are felled, logged, and transported out.

Sadly, on 2 September 2019, MFS pilot mentor and Health & Safety officer Steve Maynard (Manutuke, Rongowhakata, Ngāti Porou) passed away at his home. MFS has the video of Steve's interview for the MFS pilot evaluation, and his advice for anyone thinking about forestry:

> I'd just talk to them and say, aye (yes) it is a dangerous job if you make it dangerous for yourself. So, if you go out there and do your job properly you will get along and go home every day, every night.

The MFS pilot evaluation case study is an example of a Kaupapa Māori approach to evaluation with practical application. The research and evaluation findings contributed to the central government decision to co-fund an upscale of the programme to deliver 3 concurrent training courses in three locations by June 2020.

In response to the COVID-19 pandemic on Tuesday 24 March 2020, two local forests hosting MFS training were locked down and on Wednesday 25 March 2020 the nationwide lockdown saw all MFS training sites close. The current rookies worked online and in workbooks to complete the 'paperwork' for New Zealand Qualifications Authority (NZQA) Level 3 Forestry qualifications, their mentors continued professional development in training and teaching skills and the MFS Kaiako, Board and Directors reviewed the MFS systems and strategies.

On 28 April 2020, when the nationwide COVID-19 alert level dropped to three, the MFS programmes restarted, following existing and new COVID-19 responsive health and safety measures.

In June 2020, WorkSafe New Zealand (2020) reported from April 2019 to March 2020 that Forestry and Logging were the most lethal worksites for work-related fatalities (7) topping all sector rates at 115.06 per 100,000 full-time equivalent employees. Of the seven forestry fatalities, five were from falling objects.

In late June 2020, a 300-mm rainfall event saw slash smothering the sands of Tolaga Bay and other Te Tairāwhiti beaches with rotting wood. Lessons learnt from 2018 regulated that forestry harvesters had to stack slash away from waterways. Five companies in Te Tairāwhiti faced prosecution for breaching the new regulations. Some tangata whenua are thinking of other uses for slash including bio fuels and carbon filters.

In September 2020, the NZQA granted MFS registration as a Private Training Establishment (PTE) that can receive central government funding for training. Before granting registration, NZQA needs to be certain that the PTE will be governed and managed with integrity and will provide high-quality education and a sound and stable learning environment. This entailed a thorough analysis of the application, to determine whether it satisfied the applicable criteria or statutory requirements.

In April 2021, MFS had to pivot their delivery due to ongoing impacts of COVID-19 on their programmes and contracts. The forest-based training was changed to focus on the qualifications that cover the skills needed to be safe in the forest, ahead of placement into work in the industry. COVID-19 was a high risk that had not been anticipated, by anyone. The effects of COVID-19 were a major contributing factor in the decision to discontinue the MFS Programme.

By 2022, Te Pūkenga New Zealand Institute of Skills and Technology (no date), a new tertiary organisation, had been created to transform vocational learning in Aotearoa. The ITPs and ITOs became a single institution. Forestry training available nationwide is listed on Te Pūkenga website.

References

Aotearoa New Zealand Evaluation Association (ANZEA). (2019). *Evaluation standards for Aotearoa New Zealand*. ANZEA/SUPERU. www.anzea.org.nz/app/uploads/2019/04/ANZEA-Superu-Evaluation-standards-final-020415.pdf

Atkinson, J., Salmond, C., & Crampton, P. (2014). *NZDep2013 index of deprivation*. Department of Public Health, University of Otago. www.otago.ac.nz/wellington/research/hirp/otago020194.html

Cram, F. (2016). Lessons on decolonizing evaluation from Kaupapa Māori evaluation. *Canadian Journal of Program Evaluation/La Revue canadienne d'évaluation de programme, 30*(3) (Special Issue/Numéro special), 296–312.

Cram, F. (2018). Conclusion: Lessons about Indigenous evaluation. In F. Cram, K. A. Tibbetts, & J. LaFrance (Eds.), *Indigenous evaluation* (New directions for evaluation, vol. 159, pp. 121–133.

Cram, F., Kennedy, V., Paipa, K., Pipi, K., & Wehipeihana, N. (2015). Being culturally responsive through Kaupapa Māori evaluation. In S. Hood, R. Hopson, & H. Frierson (Eds.), *Continuing the journey to reposition culture and cultural context in evaluation theory and practice* (pp. 289–311). Information Age Publishing.

Cram, F., Pipi, K., & Paipa, K. (2018). Kaupapa Māori evaluation in Aotearoa New Zealand. In F. Cram, K. A. Tibbetts, & J. La France (Eds.), *Indigenous evaluation* (New directions for evaluation, vol. 159, pp. 63–77).

Durie, M. (1994). *Whaiora: Māori health development*. Oxford University Press.

Gisborne Herald. (2019). *Forestry pilot hailed a success* (Front Page on 2 April 2019). http://gisborneherald.co.nz/localnews/4030132-135/forestry-pilot-hailed-a-success

Irwin, K. (1994). Māori research methods and processes: An exploration. *Sites, 28*, 25–43.

Kennedy, V., Cram, F., Paipa, K., Pipi, K., Baker, M., Porima, L., & Tuagalu, C. (2015). Beginning a conversation about spirituality in Māori and Pasifika evaluation. In S. Hood, R. Hopson, & H. Frierson (Eds.), *Continuing the journey to reposition culture and cultural context in evaluation theory and practice* (pp. 151–178). Information Age Publishing.

Koia, H. (2018a, November 2). *ManaiaSAFE Forestry School pilot project status report 1 of 5 (Week 1 of the 20-week pilot training programme)*. Train Me Quality Services Ltd. https://docs.wixstatic.com/ugd/b9ddf8_e29633fcfccc4ad2b4da96c75da0f434.pdf

Koia, H. (2018b, December 7). *Status report 2 of 5 (Week 6 of the 20-week pilot training programme)*. Train Me Quality Services Ltd. https://docs.wixstatic.com/ugd/b9ddf8_38e1c42be25b4399a6e16967909495e7.pdf

Morgan, T. K. K. B. (2006). Decision-support tools and the indigenous paradigm. *Proceedings of the Institution of Civil Engineers, Engineering Sustainability, 159*(4), 169–177.

Nunns, H., Peace, R., & Witten, K. (2015). Evaluative reasoning in public-sector evaluation in Aotearoa New Zealand: How are we doing? *Evaluation Matters – He Take Tō Te Aromatawai, 1*, 137–163.

Radio New Zealand. (2019a). *New Zealand Institutes of technology 16 polytechnics to merge*. www.radionz.co.nz/news/national/382366/nz-institute-of-skills-and-technology-16-polytechs-to-merge-under-government-proposal

Radio New Zealand. (2019b). *Prime Minister Jacinda Adern outlines vision of economic growth and global challenges*. www.radionz.co.nz/news/political/382003/prime-minister-jacinda-ardern-outlines-vision-of-economic-growth-and-global-challenges

Radio New Zealand. (2020a). *Family says no justice for WorkSafe investigated workplace deaths*. www.rnz.co.nz/news/national/420300/family-says-no-justice-for-worksafe-investigated-workplace-deaths

Radio New Zealand. (2020b). *Number of work related deaths reported goes up*. www.rnz.co.nz/news/national/408058/number-of-work-related-deaths-reported-goes-up

Rangahau. (n.d.) www.rangahau.co.nz/rangahau/

Sinclair, J. (2017). *Felling the wall – An investigation into forestry training in the Gisborne Region* (Course 36, pp. 6–7). Kellog Rural Leadership Programme.

Smith, G. H. (1997). *The development of Kaupapa Māori: Theory and praxis* (Unpublished PhD thesis). University of Auckland.

Smith, L. T. (2012). *Decolonizing methodologies – Research and Indigenous peoples* (2nd ed.). Zed Books.

Te Aka Māori Dictionary Online. (n.d.). https://Māoridictionary.co.nz/

Te Pūkenga New Zealand Institute of Skills and Technology. (n.d.). https://tepūkenga.ac.nz

Tertiary Education Commission – Te Amorangi Mātauranga Matua. (2017). *Tertiary Education Report. Background for a first discussion about ITP Viability. Report Number: B/17/00875*. Tertiary Education Commission. www.tec.govt.nz/assets/Reports/2e3edec3c0/TEC-report-Background-for-first-discussion-about-ITP-viability.pdf

Treasury (2015). *Guide to social cost benefit analysis July 2015*. https://treasury.govt.nz/sites/default/files/2015-07/cba-guide-jul15.pdf

Treasury (2018a). *CBAx transforming cost benefit analysis practice*. https://treasury.govt.nz/sites/default/files/2018-06/cbax-poster-jul16.pdf

Treasury (2018b). CBAx tool user guidance: Guide for departments and agencies using Treasury's CBAx tool for cost benefit analysis September 2018. https://treasury.govt.nz/sites/default/files/2018-09/cbax-guide-sep18.pdf

Treasury (2018c). *Cost benefit analysis template – wellbeing domains*. https://treasury.govt.nz/publications/template/wellbeing-domains-template

Wilkie, M. (2010). *Te Taumata, Te Timata: The pinnacle, the first step* (Unpublished PhD thesis). Victoria University of Wellington. http://researcharchive.vuw.ac.nz/handle/10063/1426

Wilkie, M. (2018). *ManaiaSAFE Forestry School pilot evaluation: Report 1 scoping and initial review*. ManaiaSAFE Forestry School.

Wilkie, M. (2019a). *ManaiaSAFE Forestry School pilot evaluation: Kaupapa Māori social cost benefit analysis*. ManaiaSAFE Forestry School.

Wilkie, M. (2019b). *ManaiaSAFE Forestry School pilot formative evaluation*. ManaiaSAFE Forestry School.

Wilkie, M. (2019c). *ManaiaSAFE Forestry School pilot evaluation*. ManaiaSAFE Forestry School. https://931cffa0-55bc-4b66-91dd-ef185ecfa33b.filesusr.com/ugd/b9ddf8_e0ddf04b5839400fbe1d-64f3471b7ee7.pdf

WorkSafe New Zealand. (2017). *Training and workforce development in forestry*. www.worksafe.govt.nz/worksafe/research/research-reports/2016-forestry-research/2016-forestry-research-documents/2016-Forestry-Research-Report-6.pdf

WorkSafe New Zealand. (2020). *Work-related fatalities updated 2 June 2020*. https://data.worksafe.govt.nz/graph/summary/fatalities

5 The TCS School Program Evaluation

Elissa Frazier and Leanne Kallemeyn

Case Goals

Three overarching goals guided the development of this case, and we hope they also guide teaching and learning with this case. One goal was to address the challenges in navigating interpersonal relationships and addressing ethical issues, such as balancing conflicting stakeholder needs and interests. The second goal was to address the challenges in culturally responsive evaluation (CRE); more specifically, engaging stakeholders, asking the right questions, and framing the data, which all require attention to CRE principles in this context. Finally, we sought to embrace reflexivity as a professional practice and further reflect on professional growth through interrogating the American Evaluation Association (AEA) Guiding principles and AEA's Statement on Cultural Competence. I (Elissa) was transitioning from a role as a K12 teacher and instructional coach to an evaluator. As the study and practice of evaluation are intertwined, these experiences afforded me the opportunity to immerse myself in the practice-side while reflecting on how those experiences were shaping me into a new professional identity. The tangible product of this case lives as its own cultural artifact, a representation of my growth in the role of an evaluator, and one part of an ongoing conversation around reflecting on problems of practice.

AEA's Statement on Cultural Competence and Guiding Principles of Integrity, Respect for Persons, and Common Good and Equity were most relevant for the development of this case. The statement on Cultural Competence highlights the importance of evaluators respecting the culture of stakeholders, given the diversity of cultures and likelihood that an evaluator will work on evaluation settings with cultures different than their own. Cultural Competence is a lifelong process that demands evaluators practice a high degree of self-awareness and self-examination.

The Guiding Principles describe the values and guidelines for ethical conduct and behavior of evaluators (AEA, 2018).

- AEA's Statement on Cultural Competence:

  Cultural competence is a stance taken toward culture, not a discrete status or simple mastery of particular knowledge and skills. A culturally competent evaluator is prepared to engage with diverse segments of communities to include cultural and contextual dimensions important to the evaluation. Culturally competent evaluators respect the cultures represented in the evaluation. Several core concepts are foundational to the pursuit of cultural competence.

  (AEA, 2011)

- Principle C: Integrity states that "Evaluators behave with honesty and transparency in order to ensure the integrity of the evaluation." (AEA, 2018).
- Principle D: Respect for People states that "Evaluators honor the dignity, well-being, and self-worth of individuals and acknowledge the influence of culture within and across groups" (AEA, 2018).
- Principle E: Common Good and Equity states that "Evaluators strive to contribute to the common good and advancement of an equitable and just society" (AEA, 2018).

Case Narrative

Introduction

The case describes a program evaluation of a school-based equity initiative in the Midwest seeking to create an inclusive and positive school environment for all students and families. The context is a multiple case study of four schools within a public urban charter network serving culturally diverse students in ten schools. The funder intentionally chose the five person evaluation team for its diversity in experiences and expertise. However, only some team members shared the same cultural, ethnic, or racial backgrounds of most students, families, or communities where the evaluation took place. The team's social and political composition more closely aligned to teachers and administrators. The results of the evaluation were high stakes as they would inform the network's strategic diversity, equity, and inclusion goals and potentially impact funding for the equity-based program seeking to expand to all schools in the charter network. At this place in the evaluation, data collection was underway and the removal of a key stakeholder triggered staff reorganization and served as a critical event to shift power dynamics within the charter school network.

This case is fictional, yet we have grounded it in the lived experiences from a real program evaluation. We fictionalized all descriptions to protect the confidentiality of stakeholders involved. This case addresses the challenges in contextually and culturally responsive evaluation; more specifically, navigating interpersonal relationships and ethical issues, such as balancing what is good for an evaluation and how it aligns with perceptions of the greater good.

Background on Thriving Communities and Schools Collaborative (TCS) Project

The following features were central to the TCS Project:

- Five-year program funded by a local foundation.
- Provided academic, social-emotional, and cultural enrichment in after-school programs.
- Promoted parent and community engagement with family programming (e.g., GED classes, English classes, Zumba, and Technology classes).
- Provided local workforce training recommendations and health-related service recommendations to parents and families through school to community partnerships.
- Provided teacher professional development offerings for which teachers receive stipends for attending, which focused broadly on restorative practices, creating stronger school to community partnerships, and culturally responsive relationship building.
- Used seasoned charter network teachers and neighborhood residents as after-school resource coordinators and program liaisons.
- Recommended, based on network administration support, voluntary TCS professional development offerings for teachers, building administration, and school support staff to attend.

The TCS Collaborative provided programming to four out of ten charter schools within a large urban Midwest city. These schools were located within a ten mile radius across three economically challenged neighborhoods. And, these areas, which were socioeconomically, racially, and ethnically diverse at one time, were largely homogeneous now; they were home to mostly low-income African American families and a growing population of working-class Mexican Americans. Many of the families who chose to send their students to "choice" schools did so because of the decline of their neighborhood schools, lack of sufficient funding, and subpar academic readiness. This charter school network had a student–teacher ratio of 25:1 which was much lower than surrounding public neighborhood schools. Students also had 1:1 Chromebooks, substantial clubs, and after-school activities as well as access to a college-preparatory curriculum.

With school data showing that one-third of all students had received at least two suspensions, coupled with a drop in school quality rating due to a declining percentage of students "on-track" to graduate, the network began to develop an intervention strategy six years ago. Staffing in the TCS Collaborative partner schools had proven challenging as well; historically, the network had hired young Teach For America graduates who were culturally mismatched with the students they serve; and, they typically had very little teaching experience prior to onboarding. Seventy-five percent of the teaching staff left the network within three years on average, and less than five percent lived in or around the surrounding neighborhoods. For these reasons, the TCS Collaborative was hired to support their charter network initiative to create more responsive and inclusive school communities than currently existed. They were also hired to strengthen both teacher–student relationships, and school-community relationships.

The TCS Collaborative had been operating for four years and their contract was up for renewal in the fifth year. The board of directors of the charter school network was considering expanding the program to the other six schools; however, both the board and the funder needed more information to better understand the TCS program and how it served the needs of the teachers, students, and the families. The board of directors commissioned an external evaluation team from the local university to conduct the evaluation. In support of the evaluation team, four TCS liaisons and the charter network's Chief Diversity and Equity Officer were assigned to facilitate any needs as they arose. They had worked in their respective roles for the past three to four years and were trusted by teachers and building administration across the network.

Background on the Evaluation

The evaluation team adopted a CRE approach seeking to engage with a broad range of stakeholders considering their role, level of influence, and power within the schools. When developing the survey instruments and interview protocols, evaluation team considered not just qualitative and quantitative data that would best answer the evaluation questions, but were responsive in the language that they used for the specific cultural context and the types of questions they asked. To gain a more holistic understanding of the cultural and contextual factors impacting the schools and the program they were evaluating, they developed comprehensive contextual maps, researched the history of neighborhoods and surrounding communities, and tracked current events through several sources systematically over several months.

CRE and diversity lived in the fabric of the evaluation team. In forming the evaluation team, there was diversity in so many levels. There was racial and ethnic diversity with Latina and African American female evaluators alongside White male and female evaluators, place-based diversity as some evaluators were from urban cities, while others were from small, more suburban areas across the US. There was also a variance in expertise, ranging from psychology, health, K12 teacher education, and research methodology with substantial experience in qualitative, quantitative, and mixed methodologies. There was a range of research and evaluation experience, some with three or four years, others with ten to 15 years, and well-respected research scientists with over 20 years' in the field of evaluation. Most team members had done prior evaluation work focused on equity initiatives or school improvement policy. And, as a result of the rich diversity in our team makeup, each team member was expected to contribute to collaborative conversations and offer their unique perspectives, lived experiences, and professional knowledge.

The evaluators created an internal team culture that respected differing points of view and differing theoretical approaches to evaluation. Some members of the team were grounded in the transformative evaluation paradigm, believing the role of the researcher to be "one who recognizes inequalities and injustices in society" (Mertens, 2007, p. 212). Those team members were aware of power and privilege within the complex social and political realities of their work, and they placed value on building trust with all stakeholders, especially those whose perspectives historically may have been excluded or undervalued. While others did not hold the same commitment to social justice, the team greatly respected each other's differences and engaged in rich conversations in their joint work. As CRE is an approach and a lens for understanding cultural context, both the program evaluation context and the internal team context benefited from authentic and deep engagement.

For data collection, evaluators planned to visit program offerings, conduct individual interviews with teachers and building administration in participating schools, and observe a sample of classroom teachers who had participated in three to four TCS offerings. The board president selected charter network leaders to be interviewed as well. Due to time and budget limitations, the evaluation team did not collect data directly from parents and families, nor did they collect data from non-teaching staff or paraprofessionals. The evaluation team had access to secondary data from TCS program participants (teaching staff, support staff, and families) across school sites, which was collected by hand and electronic systems. These sources had only been gathered for the past two years. TCS agreed to provide the evaluation team all of their available records, which included attendance and participation data as well as more detailed participant feedback responses from handwritten exit tickets.

Evaluators embraced a CRE approach when attending to selecting and adapting instrumentation, asking the right questions, and engaging stakeholders (Frierson et al., 2002). As noted earlier, their budget and evaluation design did not allow for them to meet with students, parents, school personnel, or the full range of all instructional staff. However, they designed their site visits to interview teachers in their natural settings and attend program offerings off-site in addition to their interviews with school administrators. They also designed their survey instruments and interview protocols considering not just qualitative and quantitative data that would best answer the evaluation questions, but were responsive in the language that they used for the specific cultural context. For example, instead of using the external-facing formal name, *Thriving Schools and Communities Collaborative*, the evaluation team used the insider – community term, *Thrive Circle* when engaging with participants. Additionally, the evaluation teams' findings from their research on school neighborhoods and contextual maps informed their understanding of the people and places they were entering as outsiders.

Challenges

The evaluation team was in the midst of data collection and scheduled several site visits over a two-week time span to interview network stakeholders and to observe some of the TCS professional development offerings. During one of these visits, two members of the evaluation team met with the Chief Diversity and Equity officer to learn more about the district's strategic plan and DEI initiative and to get a better understanding of the networks' needs. At this time, the Chief Diversity and Equity officer told the evaluation team that her position had been eliminated due to budget cuts, that her responsibilities would be disbursed among other leadership, and that she would leave office in a month's time. The decision was made at the most recent board meeting earlier in the week. And, toward the end of the meeting, the Chief Diversity and Equity officer was candid with the evaluation team. She expressed concern that when she left office, the TCS partnership and other diversity programming would fall to the wayside and the cultural transformation that she believed had begun would be hindered. She feared that if the evaluation report did not show favorably in support of TCS, "much-needed student programming and family supports will be lost."

After the meeting, the evaluation team had scheduled a lunch break at a local café, which gave them a chance to debrief on the visit thus far.

EVALUATOR-1: Wow – I wasn't expecting that news from the Chief Diversity and Equity Officer. She was one of our primary users and champions of this evaluation. I have grown to appreciate and respect her work. How are we going to follow through on her request?

EVALUATOR-2: I am just glad we had that meeting and found out now. What if she hadn't shared that with us and then at our next visit she was gone?

SENIOR EVALUATOR: I have seen this happen before as turnover in these positions is all too common. I am glad we have lunch to talk about this. What are your thoughts on her request?

EVALUATOR-1: I think she is right that the partnership will fall apart, and I have said from the beginning of working with you that we need to leverage evaluations to advocate for and promote diversity. I know we have some evidence to share in support of this work.

EVALUATOR-2: I hear you, but in the analysis that we have done so far, we have seen the mixed results on impact. I am concerned that a report that only reflects favorably on TCS will not be a fair representation, not to mention that we could completely lose our credibility with the Board.

SENIOR EVALUATOR: It feels like we are between a rock and a hard place, doesn't it?

EVALUATOR-1: You could say that again.

SENIOR EVALUATOR: I am glad we are not done with our visit yet. Tonight let's see if the board meeting minutes are posted online yet and also inquire about this change during our visit. There could be several reasons for choosing to eliminate the position in budget cuts, so it would be helpful to understand the rationale. We should also review the findings we have in the preliminary report. We can use that to help us focus the data collection we are doing the rest of this visit.

The next day they resumed their school site visits, documenting a mix of evidence regarding TCS. On Saturday, the evaluation team had a chance to attend a half-day TCS offering on restorative practices. TCS staff and network school personnel gave a short acknowledgement of the evaluation team so that all the participants knew why they were there. As observers, the evaluation team witnessed facilitators sharing their own personal stories describing patterns of disciplinary interactions leading to suspensions from multiple school settings. Their stories illuminated how the schools did not serve as places to learn and grow socially, emotionally, or academically. Following their personal stories, facilitators reviewed research on implicit bias, the school to prison pipeline, and a framework for strengthening relationships with teachers and students through restorative justice tenants. The second half of the workshop focused on role-playing, practicing some of the strategies presented in the morning, and reflecting on solutions for some of the building-level structural reform. Facilitators acknowledged and answered questions that arose concerning personal challenges teachers faced when moving away from traditional disciplinary measures.

As the workshop wrapped up, members of the evaluation team were at the back of the room getting their bags and coats together before they left. Two participants began talking a few feet away, and the team saw and heard the entire conversation.

PARTICIPANT-1: Hey Joe, do you mind giving me a lift to the train station? It's not far, but I don't feel like walking. I'm exhausted. Can't wait to get outta here. *[Scratching a creased forehead]*

PARTICIPANT-2: What happened?

PARTICIPANT-1: I think the presenter had it out for me. Every time I said something, he'd have a comeback. *[Both hands in the air at chest level, pushing against invisible stop sign.]* If I hear the word "data" one more time, I'm gonna throw up.

PARTICIPANT-2: *[Looking surprised]* Really? I didn't notice. I liked hearing all the community stuff. I didn't know any of that.

PARTICIPANT-1: It was in our small group. You must have been in the other room. It was horrible. I didn't think I could be honest. I mean what do they expect? These kids are out of line and they don't respect authority.

PARTICIPANT-2: I hear you. That sounds pretty bad. I lucked out. My group was great.

PARTICIPANT-1: Wozniak told us that this one was one of the better ones. She came last month with her team, said she got a lot out of it. If she hadn't recommended it, I wouldn't have come. Thank goodness we're getting paid.

PARTICIPANT-2: Isn't Wozniak in that cohort?

PARTICIPANT-1: What do you mean?

PARTICIPANT-2: I thought she was doing the principal prep stuff.

PARTIPANT-1: Yeah, I think she is in the cohort ahead of me. I'll be done next year. Can't wait to get out of the classroom. I'll be happy when all of the TCS stuff blows over.

After the participants left the room, the evaluation team members also headed home.

When the evaluation team got together the following Monday for their regular scheduled weekly meeting, they took time to review fieldnotes and shared their takeaways from school visits, interviews, and focus groups. One of the team members who took notes after overhearing the conversation between the two teachers shared them openly. He asked the team what they thought about the interaction and how that knowledge might inform questions in the following months on their next round of scheduled visits. A decision needed to be made collectively about whether to use the data from the conversation in their reporting or not. There were implications in either decision, and the team discussed their varying points of view. One team member was uncomfortable using the data in any way; she believed that the conversation was a private exchange among two work colleagues that happened to take place in the workshop's physical space. Another team member disagreed and believed that the conversation, albeit personal, was still directly connected to the program evaluation, and that it revealed cultural aspects of the schools and gave meaningful insights into existing challenges. Given the elimination of the Chief Diversity and Equity officer and possibility that it was an early sign the board may no longer invest in TCS, such information was critical to include. Ultimately, no consensus was reached, and the team agreed to revisit the conversation the following week.

References

American Evaluation Association. (2011). *American Evaluation Association statement on cultural competence in evaluation.* Retrieved from www.eval.org/ccstatement

American Evaluation Association. (2018). *Guiding principles for evaluators.* Retrieved from www.eval.org/p/cm/ld/fid=51

Frierson, H. T., Hood, S., & Hughes, G. B. (2002). Culturally responsive evaluation and strategies for addressing it. In *The user friendly evaluation handbook.* National Science Foundation.

Mertens, D. M. (2007). Transformative paradigm: Mixed methods and social justice. *Journal of Mixed Methods Research, 1*(3), 212–225.

6 Leveraging Cultural Humility in the Evaluation Process to Facilitate the Healing of Organizational Trauma

Steven D. Kniffley Jr.

Introduction

Similar to an individual who has experienced a traumatic event, organizations can experience trauma in the form of harmful policies, siloed and exclusive cultural dynamics, and toxic personalities. Additionally, as with family members who may experience secondary re-traumatization, employees and clients can experience the inter-generational transmission of organizational trauma through mechanisms such as cultural messaging and organizational socialization. This chapter explores the evaluation of a mid-size non-profit organization committed to empowering victims of intimate partner violence, "Women's Empowerment Inc." (name changed to protect confidentiality). Specifically, this chapter highlights the process for navigating organizational trauma as a part of the evaluation procedure including (1) developing a shared language for communication and feedback via cultural humility training, (2) utilizing a mixed methods approach for evaluation (e.g., surveys, focus groups, and working sessions), (3) incorporating a participant/observer approach to evaluation, and (4) soliciting ongoing feedback about the process and outcomes. This chapter also discusses the role of culture in navigating a meaningful evaluation process when significant cultural differences exist between the evaluator and individuals that make up the organization.

Cultural Considerations

The evaluator identifies as a cisgender heterosexual Black male in his mid-thirties with a social justice-oriented faith background. The evaluator works as an Associate Professor and Chief Diversity Office at a small private university. Furthermore, the evaluator is a licensed psychologist with almost ten years of program evaluation working with school districts, non-profits, hospitals, for-profits, and law-enforcement departments nationally and internationally. The evaluator takes a culturally competent and inclusive approach to the evaluation process. Specific themes connected to this approach include transparency, collaboration, intersectionality, cultural humility, and inclusion. Utilizing a culturally competent and inclusive approach to the evaluation process allows the evaluator to flatten the hierarchy between the evaluator and the organization. Also, this approach amplifies the voice of the individuals and clients connected to the organization, enhancing the authenticity and openness of the participation in the evaluation process. Finally, a culturally competent and inclusive approach encourages evaluators to be aware of their biases and to include an intersectional lens regarding the varying cultural dynamics within the organization.

As noted previously, the organization that participated in the evaluation was a mid-size non-profit committed to empowering victims of intimate partner violence and sexual assault.

DOI: 10.4324/9780429277788-6

Women's Empowerment Inc. had been a fixture in the local community for several decades and provides several programs including a shelter for victims of intimate partner violence and their families, crisis counseling, and training and education around intimate partner violence and sexual assault. The Women's Empowerment Inc. has over 50 employees who work across 6 programmatic areas: (1) Crisis response, (2) Emergency shelter, (3) Sexual assault services, (4) Advocacy and Support, (5) Housing, and (6) Children's services. The organizational staff is predominantly White (71%), aged 25–44 (52.4%), female (84%), heterosexual (45%), and had worked at Women's Empowerment Inc. for an average of 3.9 years. Furthermore, White cisgender women hold most of the leadership positions, comprising 81% of the executive and director level positions.

As a cisgender heterosexual Black male in his mid-thirties, there were a number of cultural considerations for the evaluator to be mindful of while navigating the evaluation process with the Women's Empowerment Inc. The evaluator had to be mindful of his privilege as a cisgender male working with mostly cisgender female leadership team and staff. Within this dynamic, the evaluator needed to be intentional in regard to creating space for voice and choice. The women in leadership and the staff had presumably experienced significant marginalization by other males as they navigated both their professional and personal lives. Additionally, many of the clients supported by the organization were women who had experienced abuse at the hands of males creating an ongoing narrative related to the impact of patriarchy and male privilege in the workplace setting. The evaluator needed to conduct the evaluation process in a way that did not recreate this experience of marginalization by seeking consistent feedback, intentional and thoughtful listening, and engaging in a co-expert posture.

Additional areas of privilege that the evaluator had to be aware of while navigating the evaluation process with Women's Empowerment Inc. included the following: educational attainment, sexual orientation, and being able-bodied. As a doctoral level professor and clinician, individuals within the organization could view the evaluator as elitist or out of touch and generally unable to communicate in a manner that appreciates the perspective of leadership, staff, and the clients they serve. Additionally, as a cisgender male, the evaluator needed to be mindful in his use of gendered language and the ways he might communicate the expectation of a gender binary (e.g., male perpetrator, female victim) when exploring the organization mission, vision, and programming. Finally, as an abled bodied individual, the evaluator needed to be aware of his blind spots (e.g., ableism) in regard to exploring the inclusive nature of Women's Empowerment Inc. in the areas of access and physical/mental health stigma and well-being.

The evaluator also had to be mindful of his own marginalized experience as a Black individual supporting a predominately White leadership team and staff. Historically, society has often portrayed Black males as dumb, deviant, and dangerous individuals. Through his scholarship, clinical work, and professional advocacy, the evaluator has sought to reduce the impact of this narrative, but is aware of its ongoing perpetuation via the mechanism of systemic racism. Although Women's Empowerment Inc. is an organization committed to supporting marginalized individuals, they are not immune to the residual impact of systemic racism via microaggressions, bias, and prejudice. The evaluator needed to conduct the evaluation process in a way that drew attention to this potential dynamic in a non-defensive but assertive manner that would allow space for conversation and the development of meaningful allyship.

To effectively engage an organization in the evaluation process, an evaluator must assume a cultural humble posture that emphasizes context, collaboration, communication, and a co-expert expectation. Additionally, evaluators must be aware of their own cultural blind spots and the ways in which these areas can be influenced by the intersecting dynamic of power, privilege, and oppression. As a cisgender able-bodied heterosexual Black male, the evaluator needed to be aware of how his diversity variables might influence the data collection, interpretation, and report out process with an organization comprised mostly of White cisgender females. Steps taken by the evaluator included the following: seeking consistent feedback, intentional and thoughtful listening, and engaging leadership and staff in a non-defensive but assertive manner that would allow space for conversation and the development of meaningful allyship. As you think about your own work as an evaluator think about what steps you will need to take to create a space of psychological safety that allows your client to be vulnerable in identifying not only areas of strength but also potential areas of growth as well. Additionally, think about ways to foster awareness and understanding concerning organizational culture, the intersection between power, privilege, and oppression, and your own cultural variables. Including these spaces and areas of awareness will enhance the evaluation process and contribute to measurable and sustainable organizational change.

Questions for Consideration

What variables are salient to your cultural identity (e.g., race, gender, sexual orientation, SES)?
How might these identities influence your experience as an evaluator?
What blind spots might your salient cultural identities create that you will need to be mindful of?
How might you address these blind spots as part of your data collection, interpretation, and report out process?
How might you leverage the organization's cultural identities as an area of strength during the evaluation process?

The Evaluation Process

The evaluation process for the Women's Empowerment Inc. organization consisted of three components: (1) cultural humility training for leadership and staff, (2) listening sessions, and (3) action sessions. In meeting with the Executive Leadership team, it was communicated to the evaluator that a culture of mistrust, isolation, and divisiveness had been fostered at the organization through the experience of chronic microaggressions and burnout/high turnover. The microaggressions reported by the staff included experiences such as differing expectations for employee performance based on racial identity, subtle comments concerning the surrounding community, and differential disciplinary treatment. The staff reported that microaggressions were a consistent part of their experience at Women's Empowerment Inc. According to the leadership team, this culture had been reinforced through organizational trauma (e.g., toxic employees) and a lack of safe spaces for staff and leadership to engage in meaningful cultural communication. Given this information, the evaluator saw that it was important to create a foundation of safety and trust as a part of the evaluation process through training focused on cultural humility and engaging in difficult cultural dialogues. By incorporating this training into the evaluation process, staff and leadership would potentially be more open to sharing their experience and ideas that could help create a more inclusive, supportive, and impactful organization.

The objectives for the training included discussing the concepts of cultural humility and the steps needed to navigate difficult cultural dialogues. The training laid a foundation for constructive conversation by establishing ground rules (e.g., share not compare-where individuals agreed to talk about their experiences without feeling the need to evaluate whose experience was more difficult) that could also be used when the conversations became more challenging during the listening sessions. Additionally, the training provided opportunities for staff and leadership to learn more about the cultures of their peers as a mechanism to promote cross-cultural shared values (e.g., many of the participants had the common experience of fighting for voice and choice for themselves, their families, and clients). The exploration of shared values would be used as a reminder that the comments made during the listening sessions were coming from a shared values system even if the way in which they were being communicated were different. Furthermore, the training included a didactic highlighting the differences between cultural competency and cultural humility as well as the ways in which cultural humility is a more meaningful approach when engaging in conversations with culturally different individuals. For example, cultural competency refers to an individual's ability to apply a definitive fund of cultural knowledge to interactions with cultural different individuals (e.g., using correct pronouns). In contrast, cultural humility refers to an individual's ability to build relationships and communicate with cultural different individuals. The underlying premise in regard to cultural humility is that cultural knowledge is only half of the equation. A culturally humble posture emphasizes the importance of having an understanding of cultural context and the ability to communicate within this context (with no expectation of getting it right all of the time) as key to navigating cultural dynamics. Finally, the training discussed the four steps needed to engage in difficult cultural dialogues: (1) exploration, (2) engagement, (3) commitment, and (4) surrendering. Exploring these four steps for cultural dialogue provided a framework for the Women's Empowerment Inc. leadership and staff to operate from when attempting to share difficult feedback about the organization or to describe the various ways they had been impacted by the culture developed within the organization.

Following the cultural humility training, Women's Empowerment Inc. leadership and staff were engaged in a one-hour listening session. During the listening session, leadership and staff were asked to describe the culture of the organization as well as what cultural climate change would look like, utilizing questions that explored areas such as policies, sustainability, programs, implementation, leadership, communication, community engagement, and internal/external relationship building (e.g., what policies would need to change to create a more inclusive environment at Women's Empowerment Inc.). The evaluator completed ten focus groups with six staff members and leadership in each group for a total of 60 participants. The second component of the listening session involved Women's Empowerment Inc. leadership and staff completing a cultural climate survey.

The cultural climate survey consisted of five Likert scale questions (1= Strongly Disagree to 5 = Strongly Agree) that asked participants about their perception of Women's Empowerment Inc. as an organization that promoted a culture of equity and inclusivity for its employees and client's, was seen as a leader in the areas of equity and inclusion, supported employees who identified with marginalized backgrounds, and provided safe spaces for employees to voice concerns within the organization about equity and inclusion issues. Additionally, participants were asked to rank Women's Empowerment Inc. performance in regard to equity and inclusion in the areas of leadership, employee support, community engagement, hiring and promotion practices, and building community and communication. Participants were asked to use a ranking system ranging from 5 (very good) to 1 (very poor).

The evaluator's goal with any evaluation is to provide the organization with a tangible and understandable report that is consistent with the voice and opinions of the leadership and staff. Additionally, the evaluator's goal is provide a dynamic report that can contribute to meaningful and transformational change within the organization through policy, programming, and community building. Within this context, the evaluator includes as part of his process a mid-point check-in with the point-persons for the organization where he reviews the initial results from the data collection process. This mid-point serves as a connection between the listening sessions and/or surveys and action sessions which are opportunities to collaborate with the organization on turning the results into implementable change.

Following the cultural humility training, listening sessions, and completion of the cultural climate survey an initial report was created and reviewed with the Women's Empowerment Inc. Executive Leadership team. The report highlighted themes captured from the listening sessions and a quantitative analysis of the survey data. The purpose of the review was to share the quantitative and qualitative results with the Executive Leadership team, process the experience of the cultural humility training, and discuss next steps. A significant concern highlighted by the Executive Leadership team was the lack of applicability and poor implementation of past cultural climate surveys. As the evaluator provided feedback to the Executive Leadership team he had to be mindful to discuss what the results would mean in regard to tangible next steps. The following paragraphs include a discussion regarding the formation of the tangible next steps used to create sustainable and measurable change to the challenges and opportunities highlighted by the assessment portion of the evaluation process.

As noted previously, the next steps included the development of action sessions to translate the results from theory into practical application. The action session consisted of three objectives: (1) reviewing priorities for Women's Empowerment Inc. that were created from the survey results, listening session themes, and leadership feedback, (2) review with the participants the framework that would be used to organize the priorities into implementable goals (e.g., SMART goals (specific, measurable, achievable, relevant, and timely), and (3) apply the SMART goal framework to the priorities generated by Women's Empowerment Inc. The evaluator engaged the organization in five action session with ten participants in each session for a total involvement of 50 Women's Empowerment Inc. leadership and staff members. Following the action sessions, the evaluator compiled the prioritized SMART goals into an action plan report that was reviewed by the Executive Leadership team and distributed to staff members during an "all hands" meeting for feedback and discussion.

Questions for Consideration

How does the participate-observer evaluation process differ from traditional program evaluation?
How does the concept of cultural humility differ from cultural competency?
What does a culturally humble evaluation process look like to you
What steps might you take as an evaluator to center the voices and experiences of marginalized individuals within organizations?
How might you adjust your evaluation process to prevent your results from becoming a "document on the shelf?"

The Evaluation Results

As noted earlier, the evaluator was hired by Women's Empowerment Inc. to implement an organization wide cultural assessment initiative to enhance the ability of Women's

Empowerment Inc. to develop culturally responsive and inclusive programming and policies. The evaluator engaged Women's Empowerment Inc. leadership and staff in a two-phase process. The first phase consisted of a number of listening sessions with program leadership and staff as well as the completion of cultural climate survey. The second phase consisted of the development of initial recommendations and the facilitation of action sessions with Women's Empowerment Inc. program leadership and staff. The following paragraphs explore the outcomes of the listening sessions, cultural climate survey, and action sessions.

Listening Sessions

The evaluator engaged Women's Empowerment Inc. leadership and staff in listening sessions to explore the concepts of cultural humility, having difficult cultural dialogues, and to provide feedback about their experience related to organizational diversity and inclusion. The conversations during the listening sessions were guided by a series of questions that fell into two categories describing Women's Empowerment Inc.'s cultural climate (e.g., what themes have you noticed related to the culture within the organization and what has contributed to this culture) and envisioning cultural climate change within the organization (e.g., what policies or programs would need to change in order to create a culturally competent climate and what are some potential barriers for creating this change).

The themes noted from the listening session highlighted an organization struggling with the experience of cultural trauma that has been transmitted across generation of employees at Women's Empowerment Inc. In response to this trauma, the organization exists in a reactionary state that contributes to a misalignment in values, mission, and programming, systemic distrust, disconnection between the Women's Empowerment Inc. leadership, board, and staff, and the perception of a lack of safety and invisibility for marginalized employees and clients. Furthermore, this reactionary state also contributed to feelings of isolation for staff, a perceived lack of accountability mechanisms, transparency, and a perceived lack of organizational effectiveness regarding intra-organizational diversity and inclusion issues. Overall, the results from the listening sessions highlighted an organization that had struggled in its diversity and inclusion efforts due to unaddressed organizational trauma that had influenced relationships, programming, policies, and the effectiveness of Women's Empowerment Inc. in achieving its mission. All together, these results pointed to a significant challenge for the organization and the evaluator.

Cultural Climate Survey

In addition to the listening sessions, the evaluator also administered a cultural climate survey to Women's Empowerment Inc. leadership and staff. The evaluator administered an organization wide survey for several reasons. First, administering a survey offered an opportunity to capture leadership and staff thoughts about the cultural climate of Women's Empowerment Inc. in a confidential manner. Adding a layer of confidentiality was important due to the ongoing observations by the evaluator concerning the lack of trust between staff and leadership as well as corroboration of this observation during the listening sessions (e.g., staff comments about retaliation). Second, the survey provided an opportunity for the evaluator to capture a snapshot of the current demographics of the organization. Demographic information from the survey would allow the evaluator to examine who was represented in the organization and to compare this dynamic to the cultural issues highlighted during the listening sessions. Finally, the survey would allow the evaluator to gather targeted information regarding Women's Empowerment Inc. diversity and inclusion practices that may not have been explicit in the listening sessions.

The cultural climate survey consisted of three components: (1) a demographic questionnaire, (2) scaling questions to assess leadership and staff's perceptions of Women's Empowerment Inc. diversity and inclusion practices, and (3) ranking questions to highlight specific diversity and inclusion challenges in the areas of leadership, employee support, community engagement, hiring and promotion practices, and building community and communication. The cultural climate survey was completed by 35 Women's Empowerment Inc. leadership and staff which represented 70% of the total employee population.

In regard to demographic information, the results from the survey indicated that the average participant were White (74%), between the ages of 25 and 44 (76%), female identifying (85%), heterosexual (55%), and had worked at Women's Empowerment Inc. for an average of 4.7 years. These demographic results highlighted a fairly homogenous population whose lack of diversity (a potential limited awareness) may have contributed to being disconnected from the lived experience of marginalized employees within the organization. Additionally, the demographic results also highlighted a younger workforce in regard to years of experience at Women's Empowerment Inc. that may influence vulnerability to the generational transmission of organizational trauma, perception of ability to effect change within the organization, and the potential for high turnover within the organization that would impact employee longevity.

In regard to the survey scaling questions, the results indicated that most Women's Empowerment Inc. leadership and staff did not experience the organization as promoting an equitable and inclusive culture for its employees (29.4% Disagreed, 29.4% Neutral). Additionally, leadership and staff did not experience the organization as promoting an equitable and inclusive culture for clients (38.5% Neutral, 23.5% Disagreed). Furthermore, most Women's Empowerment Inc. leadership and staff did not perceive the organization as being a community leader in equity and inclusion with 53% of participants either Strongly Disagreeing or Disagreeing. Also, leadership and staff did not view Women's Empowerment Inc. as being a supportive organization for employees who identified with a marginalized identity with 44.12% being Neutral and 20.59% Disagreeing. Finally, leadership and staff did not view the organization as a safe space to voice concerns about equity and inclusion issues with 29.41% being Neutral and 26.47% Disagreeing.

The last component of the cultural climate survey administered to Women's Empowerment Inc. leadership and staff was a series of ranking questions to examine the organizations performance in regard to equity and inclusion in the areas of leadership, employee support, community engagement, hiring, and promotion practices. Overall, the rankings made by the leadership and staff reflected a generally poor perception of Women's Empowerment Inc. performance across all areas. Specifically, almost half of the leadership and staff reported poor rankings in each of the areas assessed by the rankings. The results from both the survey scaling and ranking questions highlighted a significant challenge for Women's Empowerment Inc. in the creation of a culturally inclusive climate for staff and clients. As reflected in the results, areas key to the promotion of organizational equity and inclusion in regard to culture creation, inclusive leadership, policies, engagement, communication, and support, were viewed as poorly implemented by employees. The experience of poor performance in these areas overlaid with limited diversity reflected in the staff and leadership could potentially create a dynamic of mistrust, lack of safety, relational silos, miscommunication, and the endorsement of a reactionary organizational posture. This dynamic could be a contributing factor to the experience of the transmission of organizational trauma reported by leadership and staff and observed by the evaluator throughout the evaluation process.

Action Sessions

As noted previously, the evaluator engaged Women's Empowerment Inc. in five action sessions to provide tangible steps to the feedback highlighted during the listening sessions and from the cultural climate survey. The creation of tangible steps was an important component of the evaluation process. A concern noted by the leadership (and shared by the evaluator) was the fear that the results from the evaluation would just sit on a shelf (similar to evaluations completed in the past). The leadership indicated that prior evaluations hadn't yielded any organizational change due to a lack of measurable, specific, and time-sensitive goals. The action sessions served as an opportunity to continue the process of collaboration with Women's Empowerment Inc. leadership and staff to create SMART goals. The following paragraphs explore the outcome of the action sessions in regard to the goals developed by the Women's Empowerment Inc. leadership and staff.

Through the action sessions Women's Empowerment Inc. leadership and staff were able to develop nine SMART goals. The SMART goals developed included the following: (1) create standing socializing opportunities outside of meetings, (2) create a welcoming environment for staff and clients, (3) create a diversity, equity, and inclusion committee, (4) increase collaboration with community partners, (5) re-imagine programs to address systemic marginalization of Women's Empowerment Inc. clients, (6) increase contact between new employees and board members with community partners and client communities, (7) develop a culture in which Women's Empowerment Inc. leadership, staff, and board members professionally know one another (e.g., board members having strong working knowledge of staff purpose and roles), (8) develop a staff selected position on the Board and leadership team, and (9) make the employee grievance reporting policy more user friendly.

Each goal created during the action sessions included a "why" component, steps for measuring progress, and a timeline for implementation and completion. For example, in regard to the creation of a diversity, equity, inclusion committee, the "why" developed by the leadership and staff was the need for an organized group dedicated to the implementation of the diversity, equity, and inclusion initiatives. Additionally, the committee would hold leadership and staff accountable for maintaining a positive cultural climate. In regard to measuring progress, the goal created by the leadership and staff provided specifics concerning committee structure, term limits, number meetings, and involvement with organization wide initiatives. Finally, the diversity, equity, and inclusion committee goal for Women's Empowerment Inc. leadership and staff included a timeline of creation and implementation of 12 months.

After conducting the action sessions, the evaluator consolidated the goals into a written plan that was shared with the Women's Empowerment Inc. leadership team during a meeting to discuss the goals and solicit feedback. Additionally, the evaluator met with the Human Resources (HR) director to discuss implementation and steps to navigate potential barriers (e.g., identifying resources, employee buy-in, timeline). Following meetings with members of the Executive leadership team, the finalized implementation plan was shared during an all staff meeting as well as via an e-mail communication from the HR director. The goal of the various meetings and communications was to increase buy-in among Women's Empowerment Inc. employees (given their significant role in the development of the plan and its implementation) and provide an opportunity for clarity concerning timeline, roles, and responsibilities regarding the implementation plan. Finally, the meetings ensured that the implementation plan would not experience the same fate as previous cultural climate evaluations due to increased transparency, collaboration, communication.

Questions for Consideration

What is your interpretation of the results from the listening sessions and cultural climate survey?

How might your salient cultural identity variables influence your interpretation of the results from the listening sessions and cultural climate survey?

What additional questions or content would you have included as part of a survey?

What evidence of organizational generational trauma is present in the results?

What methods would you use to communicate the results to the leadership team and employees and how would you address potential barriers to implementation?

How would you evaluate success of the implementation plan at a 6-month follow-up? At a year follow up?

Conclusion

The inter-generational transmission of organizational trauma refers to the experience of secondary re-traumatization by leadership, employees, and clients due to the communication of a trauma narrative via cultural messaging and organizational socialization. The experience of organizational trauma can influence employee morale, collegiality, and productivity. Additionally, organizational trauma can significantly influence the experience of marginalized employees by creating an unsafe space that is reinforced through factors such as policies, discriminatory hiring practices, and microaggressions. To address the impact of organizational trauma on cultural climate, it is important that leadership and staff develop an awareness of areas in which the trauma could be influencing diversity, equity, and inclusion efforts. Furthermore, as the leadership and staff increase their awareness concerning the cultural climate of the organization, it is important that an implementable plan of action is developed that is SMART.

The evaluator engaged Women's Empowerment Inc. in a cultural climate evaluation utilizing the following procedures: (1) developing a shared language for communication and feedback via cultural humility training, (2) utilizing a mixed methods approach for evaluation (e.g., surveys, focus groups, and working sessions), (3) incorporating a participant/observer approach to evaluation, and (4) soliciting ongoing feedback about the process and outcomes. This process yielded meaningful data from multiple listening and action sessions that highlighted an organization struggling with the experience of cultural trauma. This cultural trauma has contributed to Women's Empowerment Inc. navigating its operations and interactions with employees and clients from a reactionary state that has led to feelings of isolation for staff, a perceived lack of accountability mechanisms and transparency, and a perceived lack of organizational effectiveness regarding intra-organizational diversity and inclusion issues.

After collecting the results from the evaluation tools, the evaluator then engaged Women's Empowerment Inc. leadership and staff in action sessions to develop measurable and clear plan of action to address the challenging areas regarding the organization's diversity, equity, and inclusion efforts. From these action sessions, nine goals were developed with realistic timelines that spanned topics such as relationship building across cultures, changes to organizational structure, messaging, and board involvement.

Throughout the evaluation process, the evaluator had to be mindful of the influence of his salient cultural identities in regard to building trusting relationships with Women's Empowerment Inc. leadership and staff. Specifically, the evaluator had to be aware of how his cultural identities as a cisgender heterosexual Black male in his mid-thirties with a social justice oriented faith background would influence his creation of evaluation tools, results interpretation, and communication of feedback. Additionally, the evaluator also had to reflect on his experience of power, privilege, and oppression while working with an organization comprised mostly of White cisgender lower- to upper-middle-class women. Balancing the identification of sources of commonality while highlighting and celebrating differences proved to be a meaningful posture for building the relationship that was needed to solicit authentic feedback from leadership and staff, offering challenging critique, and working collaboratively to bring about systemic change through an implementable plan of action.

As noted prior, the evaluation process exposed significant spaces of organizational trauma and mistrust that negatively impacted the experience of Women's Empowerment Inc. leadership, staff, and clients. However, the organization was able to explore this organizational trauma and mistrust through the process of learning more meaningful cultural communication tools and using these tools to have insight-oriented conversations and facilitated action sessions. By the end of the evaluation process, leadership and staff reported feeling hopeful about the future of Women's Empowerment Inc. in regard to their ability to resolve cultural conflicts, identify sources of microaggressions within the organization, and develop, plan, and implement meaningful and culturally inclusive policy and programming.

The case study presented in this chapter has highlighted how a meaningful evaluation process that examines the impact of organizational trauma on the cultural climate of an organization must be rooted in a shared language, a collaborative and transparent process, and centered in effective and consistent communication. Additionally, evaluators must be mindful of their cultural identity variables and the ways in which they intersect with the identity variables held by the individuals providing feedback about the organization. Finally, to prevent the evaluation from just becoming another "document on the shelf," the organization must be engaged from the development of the evaluation tools to the implementation of the recommended action items.

7 The Path to the Future

Kenneth J. Linfield

Introduction to the Case

This case, like all of the others in this book, presents a fair amount of information about the evaluation being considered to help readers know important details. You will learn about the beginnings, when the evaluators learned about the program and worked with the agency staff to agree on the elements of the evaluation. You will read about how things developed, both with the program and with the evaluation. You will discover that there were a number of changes as well as important consistency over time. There will be descriptions about actions and choices by a number of those involved in the program and the evaluation. The case will conclude with explanations of the findings, recommendations, and other aspects of how the evaluation ended, and the various parties finished this particular collaboration.

One important acknowledgement – like many of the other cases in this book, the account is not an entirely factual account of the actual evaluation. First, the names have been changed to provide some anonymity. Second, some of the specifics have been simplified for the sake of a relatively short account (a full account will take more space than in this entire book). And third, other details have been modified to enhance the case for learning.

Unlike some cases, however, readers will not be asked a specific question such as "What would you do if faced with the decision to do X or Y?" Instead, I invite you to think about as much of the evaluation process as makes sense to you. Beginning students may think of one or several elements, whereas more advanced evaluators may think of a substantial number of components. As you think about these aspects, consider a variety of questions like, "Why do I think this person or these people did these things?" "What are the beneficial results of those choices?" "What are downsides to those choices?" "What are some other things that could have been done?" "What would I have done, or what would I like to think I would have done?" "What lessons can I learn from these events that might be useful in my future evaluation work?" You may well think of other questions that would lead to productive thoughts and conversations. And your instructor(s) will probably raise still other questions. One element to note is that there will be a number of details that simply describe events and developments that are not intended to be seen as problems or issues, although some readers may raise interesting points about some of them.

It may be obvious that one reason for presenting this case in this way is that questions, opportunities, or needs for decisions; recognizing that something or several things are going wrong; and many other developments do not (always) come with labels in our work or even in life more generally. Sometimes, of course, there is a clear indication of a choice – one of the program staff calls and says, "We have a problem. Should we switch to plan B or to plan C?" But especially with the choice of continuing to do what we have been doing, the specific opportunities do not always draw attention to themselves. Likewise, choosing to do something other than follow the established path is not always presented with a sign "Do you want to do this other thing?" As noted in the first chapter of this book, one extremely important skill and practice in evaluation is reflection in action – being able to think about what we are doing and have done, and then being able to evaluate those choices and decide whether to continue or to do something else. Thinking about this particular situation and reflecting on it may help you develop your ability to reflect on your own actions, choices, and thoughts in other situations. To be clear – I am sure that you already do this reflection to an important degree. The goal is to strengthen and improve your existing practice.

One further point is that although a number of the elements of various people's identities, cultures, and other characteristics have been noted, a number of the specifics of the various people involved in this case have not been emphasized. And although certain names may suggest some characteristics or identities, some of the pseudonyms may be misleading about the actual person's identity. Along with the approach that readers are invited to think about whether there are problems to be solved or decisions to be made or different directions to take, I invite you to consider your experiences with the full range of humanity. What if you were an evaluator and one of the main staff members of the agency you were going to work with primarily spoke another language than the one you speak, and the two of you struggled at times to communicate well? What if you realized that the socio-economic status of almost all clients was radically different than your own, and you began to notice that your expectations for them was making it hard for you to pay close attention to their actual experiences? As you read this case, think about how various characteristics of the people involved might explain their actions or might cause problems for the evaluation. This case may test your imagination in some helpful ways.

Beginnings

Dr. Joe Smith was preparing the PowerPoint slides for tomorrow's lesson in the doctoral Statistics course he taught at Midwest University, when there was a knock on his door. It was Dr. Carl Johnson, the chair of his School of Psychology. Although Carl was only in his second year as chair, Joe already was very grateful Carl had been chosen in the search, as Carl obviously took very seriously his role in supporting the faculty in the school rather than micro-managing their work to try to increase their productivity according to his agenda.

"Do you have some time available Thursday afternoon?" Carl asked. "The president would like us to meet with some people she knows from the Midwest Children and Family Services here in town. They are starting a big project and need a team to run the evaluation."

"Let me see," Joe replied, as he pulled out his electronic calendar. "Sure – anytime after 1:00 will work. What's the project?"

"I'll let them describe it as it is fairly complicated. That's the main point of the meeting. But it's building children's readiness for school."

"OK . . .," Joe responded hesitantly. "But I'm not exactly strong with children."

"I know," said Carl. "Don't worry – Maria will be there, too. I think the two of you would make a good pair to tackle this project."

Joe immediately felt much better. Maria had been especially welcoming when he arrived at Midwest University six years earlier, and they often talked about work – the challenges of teaching, the difficulties students faced with increasing expenses, and various University developments – as well as personal points like their own children. Maria was not much stronger with statistics than he was with children's treatment, but they worked well together, treating each other's strengths as benefits rather than threats.

Thursday afternoon, Joe arrived at the president's conference room – a much nicer setting than the musty Psychology rooms in the basement of one of the aging buildings on campus. Carl introduced Maria and Joe to Jennifer Olander and Jamal Thomas, two directors at the nearby Midwest Children and Family Services (MCFS), and after a brief explanation that this was an opportunity to talk about the program, Carl left.

The conversation moved quite quickly into a spirited discussion about the Path to the Future Project. Jennifer and Jamal were obviously very enthusiastic about what they saw as a highly innovative venture.

Jennifer began:

> MCFS has received a substantial grant to impact the Midwest City community by improving children's readiness for school for some of the most vulnerable in our area. We include a somewhat standard element by working on child-care for pre-schoolers at four of the child-care centers we provide. But we also target their families by working to build greater stability. A big problem for the children we are focusing on is that many of their families move frequently because of financial challenges. And if the family moves every year or more often, better child-care and better pre-school education never have the chance to help, because the children can only think about adjusting to a new home, a new school, and new friends.

Jamal continued,

> But we also know that standard financial classes just do not connect with most of these parents. One important reason is that they typically have too many urgent concerns to think about learning better financial habits, let alone changing their patterns of savings and spending. Another reason is that their needs are so different from one another. We can't provide a 'one-size-fits-all' program and expect it to meet more than a small minority of the parents. So although there will be common elements in the events that address finances, our approach will be coaching. We will have four coaches trained and skilled in helping the parents decide what they want to work on even if it seems to have nothing to do with finances, and then working on steps to address what the parents have chosen. These kind of approaches really seem to work in other settings, and at some point, virtually all the parents chose some financial goals. But because they have chosen them, they are much more committed and motivated to work on them.

Joe and Maria looked at each other, and Maria replied, "So you're really taking an indirect approach. You do want to work on finances, but you expect that you will do better with these parents if you don't insist on starting with finances." Joe added, "Have you heard about Prochaska's Stage of Change model?" Jamal and Jennifer shook their heads.

Joe elaborated:

> It's a fairly new idea, at least with all the names and elements. The basic point is that most people, even those that have lots of problems, do not see that they need to change. They typically just think that things will get better somehow. When folks are like that, trying to give them new skills is a bad idea – they don't think they need it. But if they begin to believe that change will help them, and then begin to think about actually

making changes themselves, that's when they are willing to talk about new skills and new approaches. Prochaska says that not wanting to change is PreContemplation. Starting to think about change is Contemplation. When people move past Contemplation to Preparation, that's when they are open to learning how to do things differently. It sounds like you're planning exactly that – helping these parents talk about what they want until they begin identifying the financial needs that you especially want to address.

"Well," Jennifer replied:

Sort of. We do very much hope that they will choose to work on finances, and we will provide financial literacy information and training at many of the meetings. But we really are committed to having the parents choose their own goals because that is the best way to help them develop a sense of control of their lives. Feeling out of control is one of the greatest causes of their instability. So if they never pick finances, we will not force them to work on finances. On the one hand, we believe is that this approach will result in more parents choosing to work on finances than if we insisted that they pick financial goals. And on the other hand we believe that those parents who do not pick finances will still pick helpful goals that will benefit their stability and their children.

"Even more," Jamal added:

This may sound crazy, but we think this approach that responds to these parents is a productive strategy in almost all settings. That is, starting with the commitment to working with other people on goals that they have a part in choosing works out so much better in the long run than holding a rigid plan. We think this is true with our parents, which is why we are developing the program this way. But this project will involve working with many different agencies. The current climate is much more contractual than collaborative. But we believe that building a collaborative culture like this will actually do the same for agencies as it does for parents. It will free them up to work together much more productively. It probably sounds grandiose, but we really see this project as our opportunity to affect Midwest City, starting with the agencies that are involved with us.

Maria and Joe looked at each other and gasped. "You're hoping that this project, focused on children's readiness for school, will transform the climate of agencies here in the city? That's a pretty ambitious goal!" exclaimed Maria. Joe just nodded. Jennifer and Jamal shrugged and laughed. "You're right!" Jennifer said. "We know we are aiming very high here."

Joe suddenly stood up and walked over to the white board, picking up a marker. "Let me see if I understand this. Your ultimate goal is children's readiness, right?" He drew a rectangle at the far right side of the board, writing "children's readiness" inside. "And you believe that better financial stability on the one hand, and better child care on the other hand, are the two main factors that will lead to better child readiness for school." He drew two rectangles a little to the left of the "children's readiness" box, then drew arrows from each of them leading to children's readiness.

Jamal replied, "Um . . ." and paused for a bit:

Actually, we think that family stability contributes to better child readiness, although financial stability is one part of overall family stability. And we don't want to forget that family empowerment is almost as important as child readiness. The whole point of coaching is to empower families, even if we hope and expect that it will pay off in children being more ready for school, especially with the improved child-care.

The discussion continued for some time, with occasional comments from Jamal and Jennifer like, "Wow – you guys really understand what we are trying to do!" Joe and Maria noted that the stages of change model was an important feature, although a somewhat complicated one. Many evaluations generally assume that things like interventions happen for a time in a program and then some good results can be seen – roughly the idea that the intervention occurs at one time or for some time, and it then leads to the good results that are seen at a later time. In this case, it seemed clear that the program assumed a cyclical approach – coaching would lead to some movement toward willingness to change, but that would lead to revised goals in coaching, which would lead to more movement, and on through a number of cycles. Still, although it would be a number of months before the final version of the impact model was agreed up, many of the elements of the model, seen in Appendix A, were taking shape.

As the conversation began to wind down, the four readily agreed that it seemed that the Path to the Future was an exciting program, and the Midwest University team seemed like a good match to evaluate the program. Jennifer and Jamal agreed to be available to answer any questions, but otherwise Joe and Maria would work with Carl on their proposal. There was a feeling of excitement and possibility as they parted.

The First Year

Over the next few weeks, Maria and Joe worked on their part of the proposal. As Carl noted, there were important elements that involved broader elements of the University, including provisions for Graduate Assistants to handle data entry and other clerical matters, as well as administrative costs. Still, Carl was very hopeful and passed along the president's comments that she heard encouraging responses from her contacts. As it turned out, for a number of reasons, MCFM decided to contract with Dr. Fred Miller and some of his colleagues at State University, the largest academic institution in the city, to conduct all the formal assessments with the children involved in The Path to the Future. Among other points, the separate team provided a clearer basis for independence. The Midwest University team would handle the overall evaluation, which would be based on assessments by the State University team.

Soon after the contract was signed, Jennifer contacted Maria and Joe to arrange for an intensive next step of learning about their program. They scheduled most of a day for a series of interviews with MCFS staff including the director of the financial services and Jose Valequez, MCFS CEO, who talked about the rationale for focusing on both child care and financial stability; representatives from various partners including the agency that would be providing the enhanced child-care training; someone from one of the banks that provided funding because of the financial training involved; the chair of the board of the foundation funding the grant; one of the coaches that was getting ready to start working with parents; and two of the directors of the community centers where the child-care facilities were located.

As they drove back to their offices, Joe and Maria marveled at the volume of information they had received. They later noted that although it had been nearly overwhelming to try to process all of it so quickly, they had also learned a great deal about the intricacies of the program. Although it helped to clarify a number of points, they were also somewhat uncertain about how to address all the elements adequately. Joe in particular noted that the hope to affect the climate of agencies' degree of collaboration would be nearly impossible to substantiate with inferential statistical analysis. They were somewhat reassured by several interviewees' explanation that a diarist, who would be talking regularly with many of those involved in the program, would be preparing an extensive narrative with actual comments. The fact that MCFS understood that these "soft" data of comments might be the only basis for evaluating any cultural change was helpful.

The first year passed fairly quickly in many ways. Margaret Plumber and another student Graduate Assistant began to work with MCFS staff on the data management system, setting up the database with a large number of variables to support the complex logic model for the program. Joe and Maria heard regularly from Jennifer and Jamal that parents with children in the child-care centers were gradually agreeing to participate in the Path to the Future project. The coaches still had relatively smaller numbers of coaching sessions, but that allowed them to build a stronger foundation of the unique form of work that fit the program's model. Training sessions with the child-care workers were going well, and observations of the child-care sites indicated that the workers were generally providing the enhanced environment that was intended.

At one point, Joe and Maria talked about some of the patterns they noticed in the program. With the exception of Jamal, who was African American, all the other staff they had met initially at MCFS and the other agencies were Caucasian. In contrast, three of the four coaches were African American as were a substantial majority of the parents and children participating in the program. In addition, one of the four centers where the program operated, where those participants met for the financial literacy classes and with their coach, was in a part of the city near a large apartment complex that was well-known for the substantial proportion of residents who were recent immigrants to America. Many of those involved there in the Path to the Future were still learning English, which posed some challenges. Maria and Joe agreed to listen carefully for any comments about race or language during their meetings and to raise relevant questions when there was a good opportunity.

There were some unexpected developments. During the year, Joe and Maria were surprised to learn that Jennifer had left MCFS. Neither then nor later did they learn any specific rationale such as whose idea it had been nor if there were problems on either side. But Jamal seemed to be addressing all the areas that he and Maria had handled, and there was no obvious reason to believe there was any particular issue to be addressed.

Joe and Maria attended the quarterly advisory committee meetings held at MCFS offices that included many of the relevant stakeholders. They began to learn the names of many of those who were more centrally involved in the project, although they found it hard to keep all of the details straight like the names of a number of agencies that were somewhat peripherally related to the project. It became clear that there was a fairly wide range of perspectives among those on the advisory committee. For example, at one meeting, MCFS staff discussed the annual intelligence and behavioral assessments of the children. The representative from an organization known for vocal child advocacy quickly spoke up, "Giving WISCs to children every year is terrible! I think that almost qualifies as child abuse!" Although the MCFS staff gently responded, "Well, remember that this is the protocol we all agreed to last year," Joe also recalled Jennifer's remark early on that this particular agency obviously believed that they were the only ones who took child welfare seriously, "They think no one cares about children as much as they care about children!" she had said.

When the data were all entered after the end of the first year, Joe began running the analyses. One immediate challenge was connecting children's data with their parents' information – there were two different systems that required connecting both elements with each other one at a time. The next challenge then appeared – although there were a moderate number of children and of adults, enough for modest statistical power, there were only a handful of children whose parents had substantially completed the measures and the same for parents whose children had been assessed.

When Joe raised the issue with Jamal, he quickly agreed to check into what obstacles there might be. But after some time, the only answer appeared to be,

> We didn't think this would happen, but it should get better this next year. Somehow folks are a little slow to get connected, but only parents with children in the childcare centers are participating, and only the children of parents who are participating are being assessed, so the groups will match once everyone is counted. I guess parents and children are just getting matched up somewhat slowly.

Trusting that the situation would improve with time, Joe analyzed children and parents separately – testing whether children were showing improvements in cognitive development and functional behavior, and whether parents were showing greater financial knowledge, progression in stage of change, and with the other measures. The results were marginally positive. Parents showed slight improvements and no declines, but the positive findings were sporadic and relatively minor effects. And although the children generally showed improvement in absolute terms, the findings were only statistically significant when slightly more liberal criteria were used than usual. That is, examining ten or more outcomes typically involves an adjustment to the usual "$p<0.05$" decision because the multiple tests actually increase the likelihood of finding "statistically significant results." Joe and Maria talked about the situation and agreed that the relatively modest number of children translated to fairly low statistical power, which meant that even moderately strong effects might still not be significant. So Joe did not apply a common adjustment, although even then, only one improvement was statistically significant.

Telling themselves that this was the first of five years, so things would get better as time went by, Joe and Maria wrote their report making as many of these weaker-than-desired findings as they could. They talked with Jamal about their findings and presented their report at the next advisory committee meeting. Committee members and especially MCFS staff seemed to agree that the data were less impressive than they had hoped, but the explanation Joe and Maria presented seemed to make sense and be sufficiently satisfying. Joe noted, however, that the State University report included a description of the standard adjustment to statistical analysis and concluded that there was no clear evidence for improvement among the children, although it acknowledged that the numbers were low enough that strong confidence was not possible.

Years Two and Three

Moving into the second year, Joe and Maria often assumed all was going well in the absence of news to the contrary. At the quarterly advisory committee meetings, reports seemed similar to the first year – enrollments continued to grow, although at a somewhat slower pace than had been hoped. The child-care worker trainings continued to be productive – replacement staff were learning to fit in with the others, and those already trained were being refreshed as well as given new information and practice with skills. Coaching was becoming well-established with mostly full schedules, and participation reached a level that supported groups of parents at each center meeting regularly.

There were occasional distractions. As noted earlier, one of the centers was located close to a large apartment complex that commonly served recent immigrants. An enduring issue at the center was the substantial number of foreign languages that their clients spoke. The need for translators meant that costs for the center were greater per client served than at other centers, which led to repeated conversations about what level of financial support among the various centers was fair. The director of that center occasionally referred to elements like fundings in ways that could be interpreted as an accusation of discrimination on the basis of race. Although his comments were sufficiently vague and discussions quickly moved on to other topics, meetings when he was present had an extra edge of apprehension, and staff members sometimes mentioned his name with hints of exasperation – always in settings with relatively few people around, and never when he was there.

Joe and Maria decided to take a low-key approach to this situation, thinking that a more direct approach might raise defenses and yield less helpful information. When they raised the director's comments and how he was received by the other staff and agencies, as well as trying to build on any comments about race and international status, they consistently heard what seemed like open responses that people generally liked the director, but felt he was too willing to use any excuse to increase his center's resources. Staff also noted that racial and cultural issues were obviously important challenges, but they felt MCFS was clearly committed to working hard for sensitive and appropriate relations among clients and the staff at the centers. Maria and Joe agreed that there was no obvious problem they could address, but also agreed to continue to pay attention.

Toward the end of the second year, Jamal noted that he was leaving MCFS to take a faculty position at Midwest University. Maria and Joe were delighted to have him join the University as a colleague, but they wondered how the Path to the Future would be affected. Shortly after the announcement, however, they were introduced to Sally Jones who was taking over Jamal's responsibilities. Sally was friendly, engaging, and had strong credentials in work with and advocacy for children, so it seemed that the main elements were covered. Even in the short time before the annual report and meeting to discuss it, Joe and Maria had several interactions with Sally that suggested she would be a fine successor, although Jamal's departure left no African Americans among the upper-level administration at MCFS involved in the Path to the Future.

Joe was disappointed to discover that the situation with data was not much better than after the first year. As before, there were still only modest numbers of cases of both children and adults. Although there were more actual participants, many of them were missing at least some of the measures, so the number with complete information was not much better. And the disconnect between children and parents continued – there was actually a majority of each set who had no corresponding participant – children without parents' data and parents without children's data. As there were still not enough for meaningful analysis of parents and children together, Joe proceeded with each group separately – telling himself as he had the year before that things were going to improve eventually.

As with the first year, the results were in the right direction but not strong enough for traditional strict analysis approaches. If the two positive results for children had been the only two examined, they would have been strong enough, but cautious analysis (and statisticians tend to be nothing if not cautious) would report that these were only suggestive trends, not actual findings, when all of the outcomes were being analyzed together. Still, Joe and Maria again discussed their options for some time, finally concluding that they would report these two as sufficient evidence for positive results, based on the low statistical power of the sample.

At the advisory committee meeting, Joe and Maria presented their findings, only to hear Dr. Fred Miller and the State University team report that none of the differences were statistically significant. Although no one raised the discrepancy in the meeting, Joe felt very uneasy about the disagreement in the respective reports. He raised the point with Maria later, and after agreeing that it was a problem, Joe finally said, "Why don't I get together with Fred and talk about this issue?"

Joe e-mailed Fred and, in an effort to set the stage for a lighter discussion, suggested they have coffee to get to know each other better, given their common involvement in the Path to the Future project, explicitly offering to treat. When they met, Joe introduced the time as an opportunity for them to get to know each other. He deliberately focused on broader issues, asking about Fred's progress in his department and about good things as well as problems at the larger University, telling stories about humorous aspects of statistical analysis (not an easy task!), and concentrating on common academic challenges like students who do not want to work hard. Although Fred was a bit wary at first, he seemed to relax as time went by. As the conversation was winding down, Joe acknowledged that they had come to "slightly different" conclusions about the data and asked if they might talk later about how to address those issues in the future to be able to give a consistent message to MCFS. Fred replied that he would be open to such a conversation, as long as he could involve his colleagues at State University. Joe acknowledged that their primary colleagues at both universities should certainly be involved.

The "meeting" happened primarily by e-mail as they began to get close to the next annual report. Fred's main colleague, also an Associate Professor at State University, seemed especially concerned about how the two teams could resolve the differences between their approaches. Maria suggested that one approach would be to issue a single report that acknowledged each approach, the rationale for each choice, and the findings of both. While maintaining their preference for the stricter analytic method, the State University professors acknowledged that there was an understandable basis for the way the Midwest University team chose to balance the limited statistic power with standard probability tests. The actual exchanges as the deadline for the report approached still reflected their differences, but with some give and take on both sides, a single report was issued.

Several months before the annual report, Margaret Plumber and the other Graduate Assistant that year conducted several focus group meetings with parents involved in the Path to the Future project. Fred accompanied them to one of the meetings to have first-hand experience with the participants. The conversation was striking. After getting things started with introductions of those present and explanations of how the meeting would proceed, Margaret asked, "So how, if in any way, are things different for you because of Path to the Future?"

One of the men present jumped right in.

> I don't spend weekends at the bar anymore! I was talking with Adrienne about how I want to have my own place before too long. We looked at the numbers together – my income and how I spend my money – and I realized that if I keep drinking at the bar every weekend, I'll never save enough. So that week, I quit going. I'm going to have a place for my son and me, even if I have to never drink another drop.

Others told similar, if slightly less dramatic stories of recognizing, generally for the first time, the financial effects of their choices.

Margaret continued, "So when you face some of these challenging decisions, who do you talk with?" One of the women laughed and said,

> I talk with my group in the project. I don't ever talk with my other friends about money anymore. If I said I wanted to buy something I didn't need, they would tell me to go

ahead. They would lie and say it won't matter. But when I talk with my project group, they tell me the truth. They say, 'You don't need that. It's selfish for you to buy it. It will ruin your plan. So don't do it!'

Later, when Joe told Maria what he had heard, they basically gasped together at the level of change these stories represented. And Joe noted that, with regard to their vague un-ease regarding ways that racial and cultural matters might be interfering with the program, the participants in the focus group represented all the major racial groups involved in the project, and their enthusiasm especially for their African American coach made it hard to conclude that there were major problems with cultural insensitivity.

But when Joe analyzed the data and saw the earlier pattern continue of positive but relatively mild changes across the board, they puzzled over the results. The stories suggested surprisingly strong effects, but the analyses based on the measures showed at best faint echoes of those effects. It was challenging to know how to put the two results together.

One of the potential explanations seemed to be the continuing problem of missing data. In theory, all of the parents should have been paired with at least one child in the child-care center, so the elements like changes in parents' financial literacy could be correlated with changes in their child's or even children's assessments. But relatively few parents' scores could be connected with the children's assessments.

There were a number of reasons for these problems, although understanding the various issues did not solve the problem of too few cases. A fair number of parents did not have any data. When the coaches were asked why this could happen, they noted that the coaching model required them to take the parents' expressed needs as the top priority. Many of the parents would plan to answer the formal questions at a scheduled meeting only to arrive, talking about some sort of crisis like needing to move or change jobs or address a sudden health issue. Although it seemed unlikely that most parents would have a good reason not to complete their assessments, the coaches steadfastly maintained that, in fact, such emergencies were one main reason there were so few responses. On the other side, although the State University team worked hard to assess every single child in the centers, absences and partial assessments and other exceptions grew into the rule, so the number of cases remained well below all initial expectations.

Still, in particular, Joe raised the point with Sally, noting that she was in a better position to address the way those across the program addressed the issue. Sally agreed to talk with others. But when she got back to Joe a few weeks later, she said that the staff had all agreed that shifting to a greater emphasis on completing the measures would undermine the constantly repeated commitment to following the participants' needs and preferences. They recognized that such an approach risked low numbers of cases, and they believed that risk was better than changing their frequently stated approach. Joe acknowledged that his preference for greater statistical power was only one of many values, although he worried that the choice might become a problem later on.

With multiple years of the program, the cases did begin to add up, so the analyses were based on more participants than in the first year. But the large expected jump did not pan out. And the results, while generally positive, still did not reach the hoped-for strong effects. Although there were a few more significant results so the united report from the two university teams noted that there were either three or four aspects of sufficient evidence, they also acknowledged that these findings were relatively modest support for the success of the program. Both groups framed the various results in as positive a way as possible while sticking with the evidence. Joe and Maria emphasized the comments in the focus groups, feeling confident that they represented meaningful change for the parents that was not reflected, at least as strongly, in the measures. The State University team noted that the children's scores were substantially stronger than a random sample of the population, even if the particular children had not increased their scores more than modestly. Still, the advisory committee and the MCFS staff seemed pleased with the results, and the evaluation teams saw no reason to suggest major changes other than continued efforts to fill in the missing data gaps.

Bringing Things to a Close

In the final year, although the project continued roughly as it had before, it was also clear that the initial enthusiasm was beginning to wear down a bit. One of the family coaches left fairly suddenly for another job offer, and it took some time to replace her. The Graduate Assistants and coaches commented every now and then about the high pressure from MCFS staff to get parents to complete the measures, and that there was some backlash, noting the inconsistency between saying that parents' needs and interests always came first and the constant insistence on completing measures. Joe thought privately that Sally's insistence the year before on the choices of the participants was beginning to weaken, but he also felt it was too late to push for a different direction.

When Joe examined the data, he saw indications that some participants had responded without careful thought, such as when every answer was "Always" or "Never." Although a few of the cases could thus be removed, he worried that there were other cases with similar but less obvious patterns that would weaken any findings. He and Maria talked about their options and settled for only ignoring the examples with quite blatant problems and acknowledging the challenge in their written report.

As the time for the final annual report drew near, Sally began e-mailing Joe and Maria with reminders of the report's deadline with what seemed to them a different tone than in the past. Previously, Sally had made a fairly emphatic point that the evaluators were independent, and while she had a few suggestions for elements like the format, she wanted to honor their objectivity. This year, some of her requests seemed to skirt the line if not cross it of telling them what the report should say. To be fair, the most problematic elements could only be inferred when reading her e-mails a certain way. But it was enough of a change that Joe and Maria had a couple of conversations about what to do. When a meeting of the Midwest Evaluation Team and key MCFS staff was set for two weeks before the final advisory committee, they agreed that Joe would ask Sally to meet individually with her after the meeting to talk about their concerns.

The larger meeting went well enough, with Sally and others expressing their concerns that this final report would affirm the value of the project, and Joe and Maria balancing their generally positive findings with the weaker-than-hoped levels. Joe's meeting with Sally afterwards, however, began rather awkwardly. He expressed his and Maria's experiences with Sally's requests, and Sally seemed very quickly to get quite defensive, saying that she was only trying to get good value for the agencies' money.

Joe quickly shifted to another approach, saying that he was not accusing her of anything, but that he and Maria had strong reactions to some of the messages, and he wanted to share those reactions with Sally. He reaffirmed the good relations they had enjoyed since Sally joined MCFS, and so he and Maria wanted to make sure they finished out their work in a good way. Sally began to relax a little, admitting that she felt rather nervous about how the final meeting would go. Although she did not apologize for her more assertive e-mails, she did acknowledge that they might have seemed like a contrast from previous years. The conversation became much less confrontive, even almost friendly, as they began to recount some of the positive experiences they had shared as well as the productive work on the project. By the time Joe left, he was feeling much better.

The final meeting was rather anti-climactic, given the concerns that Joe and Maria had discussed now and then. Fred Miller and the State University team emphasized that the assessments showed a strong majority of the children were within the "ready for school" range that the literature described. Joe wondered privately about the exact basis for that claim, suspecting that the team had found a somewhat indirect way to approach the data, but he said nothing during or after the meeting, even when Jose Valequez made a big deal of the claim when he summarized the project at the end of the meeting. The representative from the foundation that had made the largest contribution to the project responded that he and the foundation were pleased that their money had been used so well.

Joe and Maria said their good-byes to the various staff and others that they had worked with for five years. They were pleased and relieved that things had worked out so well. But they felt some sense of loss, knowing they would no longer have regular connections with most of those involved.

Cast of Organizations, Programs, and Characters

Midwest Children and Family Services (MCFS) – A non-profit agency that provides a wide range of services for children and families. It is also known as a strong advocate for expanded services for children and families in the city and nearby region.

Midwest University – a small, private University with doctoral programs in several disciplines. Midwest University has a long history of involvement in social justice work. The new president at Midwest U. had recently made connections with several staff members at MCFS, which led to Midwest U. being considered as Program Evaluators.

State University – a large, public University with demanding standards for promotion and tenure for faculty. Two faculty members of the School of Social Work oversaw the assessment of children in the Path to the Future program on the various outcome measures of intelligence and behavior.

The Path to the Future – a five-year program designed to increase children's readiness for school through improved child-care and increased family stability.

Dr. Joe Smith – Associate Professor of Clinical Psychology at Midwest University, with expertise in Statistics and Research Design. Dr. Smith oversaw all the statistical analysis of the children's outcome measures as well as the large number of variables concerning families.

Dr. Maria Rodriquez – Associate Professor of Clinical Psychology at Midwest University with expertise in Diagnosis and Treatment of Children. Dr. Rodriquez oversaw the many discussions and negotiations about details of the trainings for child-care workers as well as the literature reviews in the annual reports.

Dr. Carl Johnson – Associate Professor and Chair of the School of Psychology at Midwest University. Dr. Johnson made the initial contact for Drs. Smith and Rodriquez with Jennifer Olander and Jamal Thomas. He also oversaw the provision of Graduate Assistants and other resources for the evaluation.

Jennifer Olander – Director of Children's Programs at MCFS.

Jamal Thomas – Director of Outreach at MCFS.

Sally Jones – Director of Children's Programs at MCFS – successor to Jennifer Olander and Jamal.

Jose Valequez – CEO of MCFS. Jose had been the author of the grant application to a local foundation that provided the primary funding for Path to the Future, as well as soliciting supplemental funding from a range of local businesses.

Dr. Fred Miller – Associate Professor of Social Work at State University with expertise in Research Design.

Margaret Plumber – Doctoral Student in Clinical Psychology at Midwest University – Graduate Assistant for the Path to the Future.

Adrienne Jones – One of the family coaches in the Path to the Future project.

Appendix 7a

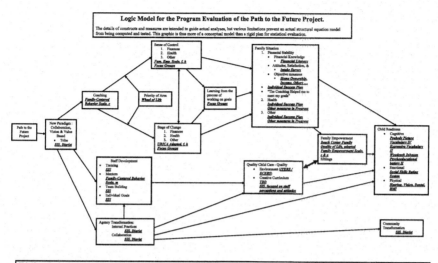

8 Reflecting on the Cases and Looking Ahead

Steven D. Kniffley Jr. and Kenneth J. Linfield

Thinking About What You Have Learned

In many ways, this chapter is anti-climactic, because the earlier chapters have already presented the substance of this book – the details of a range of evaluation cases. These concrete examples have illustrated important evaluation concepts such as working with stakeholders, devising an appropriate strategy for analysis of data, and adapting to changing circumstances, among others. Furthermore, the cases have presented readers with questions or challenges to solve. Some have been explicit by raising the question, "What would you do at this point?" Others have implicit challenges such as explanations of the evaluators' choices and thinking that can invite readers to consider whether they would have made different choices or thought differently about the evaluation.

But following the important points about reflection introduced in the first chapter, we invite you to reflect on what you have read and learned through this book by reminding you of a number of important points. Also in keeping with another point, we introduced in the first chapter, learners are different from one another. So some of our suggestions for reflection will make perfect sense for many of you and be productive, but they will not match others. Likewise, others of our suggestions will connect better with the second group but not with the first. We trust that you will take what you find useful and pass over points that are not helpful at this point. Of course, it is possible that you may return to this book at some point and find that those other ideas have become more relevant at another time or in another set of circumstances.

Signature Pedagogy

Describing the use of cases in teaching evaluation as a "Signature Pedagogy" is a somewhat fancy way to make a relatively basic point – that the specific details of an actual evaluation provide not just a fairly good but an essential component for students of evaluation to learn vital elements. To phrase it somewhat differently, we suspect that all evaluators would acknowledge how they have learned many of their most valuable lessons by doing evaluations. (Of course, some of the best lessons are when we make mistakes and learn not to repeat those mistakes in the future.) Many of you will find exactly the same, that "on-the-job training" is typically much more powerful and enduring than classroom learning. But if it is not obvious, it is very difficult, if not impossible, to get that real-live experience in most classrooms. Instead, reading cases that present vicarious experiences of evaluations is one of the best ways to bridge the gap between learning abstract concepts and actually engaging in evaluation work. And along the lines of the above point about mistakes, reading genuine cases that include elements like mistakes allows students to learn from those mistakes without having the full consequences of them.

So we invite you to reflect on some of the ways that these cases have complemented or supplemented your other learnings about evaluation. You probably had learned many important aspects of evaluation before you started this book, so you already had a good framework of understanding about the field and about the profession of evaluation. But we hope that these cases contributed to your learning in a number of ways.

How did one or more of the details help you understand various concepts? How did they add to your picture of important evaluation elements? How they modify your understanding? For example, how did you feel and what did you think when Dr. Marg considered withdrawing from the evaluation because of her medical condition? When Dr. Soprannome worried about how the evaluation might turn out, did that make you more or less interested in entering the uncertain world of real-life evaluation? You probably had a number of new insights, both comfortable and uncomfortable, as you read about these cases. What notes might you write to yourself to build on those ideas?

Teaching and Learning

We raised the point in Chapter 1 that effective teaching and learning happen when the interactions of many factors are taken into account. There is no single, perfect lesson because what works well for one student will not work as well for all students. One important element is the level of the student – beginning students need to learn the basic concepts whereas advanced students learn other things like how various concepts are related and affect one another. Presenting only basic concepts to advanced students will generally be boring, whereas addressing sophisticated interactions among disparate elements will only confuse most novices. Likewise, the nature of the curriculum is an important factor. If students are in the "Needs Assessment" course of an Evaluation Program with ten sequential courses, they should be focused much more on that component than students who are in a single "Evaluation Survey" course in a program with a very difference emphasis.

We invite you to think about how the cases in this book match your level of learning and how to think about elements that are not a perfect match for your current level. If you are early in your evaluation training, what were some of the most helpful points that reinforced and added to your introduction to the field? What were some of the pieces that are likely to be more helpful later in your training? Are there some elements that are include some aspects of both? If you are more advanced, what basic elements were helpful reminders of foundational points that you could attend to quickly and then pass by? What points were so obvious that you could skip over them? What were the more complex insights that took some pondering? What aspects of your own experience did you recall as you read some of the cases that brought back some of the challenges you have faced in the past? Were there points that seemed confusing, and that you might ask an instructor or others for help in applying to your situation?

We likewise invite you to consider the larger curriculum of your program in addition to whatever course you may be taking now. What elements of these cases were especially relevant to your current study? What components will be even more relevant in another course or at another point? Especially for students in programs that are not primarily focused on evaluation, what are some insights that you gained from these cases that apply to the direction of your program? For example, many Clinical Psychology programs include some training in evaluation, and many of the principles of evaluation, especially dealing with stakeholders, are relevant to working with clients, the staff at mental health care agencies, and other colleagues. Those in other programs may see similar kinds of applications.

In addition, what details of the different evaluation cases reminded you of the wide range of differences in your field? How does it help to remember that there are times when you will be able to give clear directions to others and other times when you mostly need to follow orders? When has your association with others on the project been a strong asset and when has it been a liability? When have you felt so comfortable with colleagues that you could relax, and when have you been highly attuned to every little nuance of communication to make sure progress is not derailed?

The Culture and Other Characteristics of the Evaluand

You saw repeatedly through the cases in this book that specific aspects of the people involved in the programs that were evaluated were extremely important for the evaluators to understand and to address in appropriate ways. Kniffley's account of repeatedly attending to various realities among the clients and staff at Women's Empowerment Inc. highlighted a number of critical elements to consider when working with a program, such as people's gender, race, education, socioeconomic status, and experiences like being abused.

When has it been especially easy for you to understand other's perspectives, and when has it been particularly difficult? How did the cases remind you of important insights you have already gained about working with others – how to pay careful attention to important aspects of their identity and how to listen carefully to learn how they are both similar to and different from others you have known in the past? How did the cases suggest new ways that you might work with others in the future, especially those who have important differences from you? What resources might be helpful ones to help you become even better at working with others?

What are some of the more obvious differences that you might encounter in working with others? How might you continue to learn more information about those differences and their implications for how people think and act? What are some of the less obvious differences you might encounter? What are some good approaches either to notice those differences or to learn about whether or not those differences are relevant?

The Culture and Other Characteristics of the Evaluator

Just as teaching and learning are intricately connected, somewhat like two sides of the same coin, the culture and other characteristics of the evaluand do not exist in isolation from the culture and other characteristics of the evaluator. In a similar fashion to teaching and learning, the responsibility to address the various elements and how they match or do not match lies primarily on the side of the teacher and of the evaluator. It is not clients' responsibility to learn academic jargon, for example, so the university professor evaluating their program will easily understand their comments. Rather professors need to recognize that a number of their habits including language may serve as an obstacle to good communication with program clients, and as evaluators, it is their job to adapt as well as they can to those being evaluated.

One important challenge, of course, is that almost all of us notice characteristics of these differences more easily in others than in ourselves. So the idea of paying attention to characteristics of the evaluand comes a little more easily to many than carefully seeing and understanding our own characteristics that may affect how others see us, think about us, and relate to us. As with many of the points in this book, we are sure that readers have already considered a range of aspects of their own identities and experiences as well as how to take them into consideration when working with others. Still, we expect that some points in these cases raised new insights and reflection on how your own characteristics may be particularly relevant to your own evaluation work.

We invite you to consider what elements of your own life might be expected to affect your work as an evaluator most powerfully? Think of the broad expanse of human differences: age, gender, race, sexual orientation, ethnicity, socioeconomic status, education level, and more. What have been some of the most productive experiences you have had of working with those who are different from you on some of these dimensions? What have been some of the most challenging experiences you have had of working with those who are different from you on some of these dimensions? What examples in the cases suggest new ideas or approaches that you might use in the future? What examples in the cases suggest that finding resources to help you feel more comfortable and more confident in working with other might be a good plan?

Both/And

One important point made both explicitly and implicitly through the book is that many of us are accustomed to thinking only in mutually exclusive categories, although there may be many other possible choices. For example, students often learn about analysis of data and think that either quantitative or qualitative approaches are possible, but assume that the choice of one precludes the other. Although the idea of mixed methods, which include both, is present in the research design literature, it somehow does not always make its way into courses and students' imaginations.

What examples in the cases gave you ideas of how you might make a choice for two seemingly incompatible options, at least to some degree? What are some of the areas where you find it difficult to reconcile two or more elements? What are some new habits you could adopt, such as when you find yourself thinking that you must choose between options, that you ask questions instead? What are some helpful questions along those lines, like, "What other choices might be possible?" "How do you see that working?" "How can we accomplish more of our goals rather than only a few of them?"

Reflection

Although this chapter is obviously focused on the specifics of reflecting on the cases in the book and the many learnings readers have gained from them, we hope that the various points raised in this book have encouraged you to find the appropriate ways to include more reflection and more helpful reflection in the full range of your work. Many Clinical Psychologists and other counselors have noted that attending to the process of a given interaction – the way that things develop rather than just the specific things that are said and done – is a critically important component of working with others in general and conducting therapy in particular. Although attention to process can be overdone, for many people, it is actually an underutilized skill, partly because most of us have difficulty paying somewhat objective attention to our own patterns.

But it is enormously helpful for evaluators (and most everyone else) to develop the skill of recognizing the ways we approach our work, those we work with, and especially those difficult times of confusion, disagreement, or conflict. For example, many of us tend to follow a given strategy almost all the time when we disagree with other. Even if we think that such a strategy is often a good one, it can be very useful to consider under what circumstances we might want to choose a different strategy, rather than responding out of habit. It is not always easy either to notice our patterns or to change them, but such flexibility is one of the skills of advanced evaluators.

Relationships

Although there were few if any explicit references in the cases to the need for good evaluators to have strong relationship skills, we hope that the point was still fairly obvious from the various accounts. Even just with regard to just the matter of working with other people, good relationship skills are essential for evaluators. Even more, when there is conflict, whether it is relatively severe or a milder level, evaluators who are able to respond to challenges nondefensively, who can work with others despite disagreements, and who can restore positive patterns of cooperation following some disruption will be much more successful than those who argue, who react defensively, or who accuse others of causing problems. Evaluators almost always begin a project by talking with staff, asking questions, learning about the details, and then negotiating the terms of the evaluation. Although some people may prefer the phrase "coming to agreement," in fact, the idea of negotiating is a good reminder that what is involved is having at least two sides reach a common understanding, which generally requires some give and take on both sides.

Far more than just coming to agreement about the overall terms of the evaluation, evaluators require good relationship skills across all of the elements of an evaluation. As we suspect readers have already learned, although the idea of an evaluation that will help programs do better is a positive thing in theory, many people, especially the staff in agencies that conduct programs, view evaluations with a fair amount of fear and trembling. "Being evaluated" makes many people worry that they will be assessed as performed at lower levels than expected and will lose their jobs. Even if people do not precisely think they will be fired, there are many other ways that their jobs could change in unpleasant ways. They could be required to be more productive, to make changes that they think will hurt their clients, or just to do new things that they would rather not do.

We hope it is clear that simply telling staff, "We're good people and we're here to help!" is almost never enough to allay their fears. Building trust takes time. There are many elements in evaluation that are sensitive in various ways, and even when the points that are sensitive are not threats to the person talking, it takes good relationship skills to help that person talk about them in productive ways.

All of this is to note that an important aspect of these cases has been the way the evaluators made their way through the interpersonal challenges of their evaluations. All of them experienced conflict between a number of their values such as good statistical findings and inferences vs. the realities of potential participants choosing not to respond for various reasons. A very common conflict is between swifter completion of the evaluation and more comprehensive work, as is between limited resources of time and other matters and covering everything that might be relevant to the evaluation. Finding the best solution that accommodates both elements of the conflict and especially helping the others who are involved in the evaluation agree to that solution is another example of the need for good interpersonal skills.

Conclusion

As we have noted, thinking back on the various points you have learned from these cases and reflecting on how they can help you become an even better evaluator is a way to deepen the

Reflecting on the Cases and Looking Ahead 93

value of this book. Many of these reflections will be cyclical – starting with one level, but building over time as you also gain more real-world experiences. We trust that this book will be one element among many that guide you toward greater evaluation excellence.

We also finish with a reminder that our progress with this book intertwined with the development of the CASE Collaborative. We have greatly benefited from their work and have been blessed with the contributions of several of their members, so we also want to remind you to follow their developments in the future. We are confident that they will continue to provide valuable insights and approaches that will also help you grow toward greater evaluation excellence. Thank you for making this book another element in your education.